advance praise

"Megan's choices are not always the wisest but she deals bravely with the consequences and once found her truth in the steam from a cup of Darjeeling tea. A beautifully written story, shocking in its tales of rejection, cruelty, and love."

> — Sandra Dutton, author of *Mary Mae and the Gospel Truth*

"Megan Madramootoo tells an authentic story of "growing-up-woman" and motherhood. Her bumps in the road read more like "six-feet-under-buried-alive." I encourage readers to follow Megan's journey through to the end to witness how she "comes of age" and learns to live!

> — Traci D. Williams, librettist, "Wailing at the Moon" (2022)

not you

not you

a memoir

Megan Harris M.

Apprentice
House Press
Loyola University Maryland

First Edition

Hardcover ISBN: 978-1-62720-531-3
Paperback ISBN: 978-1-62720-532-0
Ebook ISBN: 978-1-62720-533-7

Design by Claire Marino
Editorial Development by Jacqueline Goldman
Promotional Development by Ariana Mera

Published by Apprentice House Press

Apprentice
House Press
Loyola University Maryland

Loyola University Maryland
4501 N. Charles Street, Baltimore, MD 21210
410.617.5265
www.ApprenticeHouse.com
info@ApprenticeHouse.com

Contents

Dedicated to the younger me. Oh, the secrets I would have told you if I could, as you managed this incredibly ugly, but beautiful journey.

And to the women who are brave enough to forge their own paths, despite what the world may tell them.

But before you do—and as you do—love yourself first.

"Pretend"

It may have been 'just a kiss' –
But in that gentle pause of time, in that subtle space of bliss–
Two worlds came together, and never made a miss:
The real and the ideal, the latter remaining remiss.

And every fantasy came true,
Every dream saw the nighttime through...
Every wish was left to pursue,
And every desire had room to brew–

In that gentle pause of time, where ideals knew no end,
True love could finally be found, for as long as you let me play
pretend.

Preface

Hi Andrew. I know it's been a while, and please, I don't mean any disrespect. It's been on my mind for a long time, and I just want to ask you for your forgiveness for what I did so many years ago. I was young and my mother and I were on bad terms, and...it doesn't even matter... But I'm so glad to see that you're happy with your family because you deserve it. Take care.

-Megan
1 November 2020

My fall into the abyss that would hold me captive for some years to come all began with the abortion I had on the 21st of December 1997. I thought long and hard about whether or not to include this very intimate detail in this book; in fact, I had initially decided *against* it. However, one rare quiet evening in the present time brought back the memories of that cold day from nowhere. I cried myself to sleep that night, squeezing my eyes shut in an effort to black out the horrible recollections that got me here. Two days later, I would send Andrew the message above through *Facebook Messenger*, and give a proper apology to a good man who had been in my life some 23 years ago, finally finding closure to a chapter that had been killing me for so long.

• • •

I was 17 when I met Andrew Allen. Our eyes made contact on the Metrobus one day after it made its regular stop at New Carrollton Station, a transfer hub for those passengers who needed to pass on to other buses or catch departing Amtrak trains. I was taking the T12 home after the school day ended and his black *Maryland Terrapins* backpack hanging from one lean shoulder caught my attention. Somehow, some way, he and I struck up a conversation during our ride to our respective neighborhoods, even though he was incredibly shy. I mean, *incredibly shy*. He was a loner who had, maybe, *one* friend that I knew of, and social gatherings made his thin body twitch with nervousness and his reserved voice shake with apprehension. Always maintaining military silence, I think he would have preferred *invisibility* even if he could've found a way to master it. But he was brilliant—a junior at the *University of Maryland College Park*, majoring in business and minoring in political science, working to ascend to the top of the corporate ladder with his part-time employment at Morgan Stanley Dean Witter (even though his ability to communicate with his clients, considering his *in*ability to effectively communicate with anyone else, completely baffled, but amazed me).

He lived one bus stop after me, less than a mile away from my mother's complex. We talked on the phone every evening after school, but were never able to date as much because my mother, Veronica, was determined to make an impossible living situation for my last years of school. We had never seen eye to eye for as long as my memory could retain, so I had to sneak around most times to see him. Anyway, Andrew was (not surprisingly) a virgin, and during our very first time together, I got pregnant. He was supportive—even bought the pregnancy test and stood outside the door to my mother's house while I peed on the stick upstairs in the bathroom. I was floored when the positive results appeared almost immediately, and just as quickly, we decided to terminate the pregnancy.

I slipped into a helpless depression as I anxiously awaited to get rid of my burden. Continuously nauseous...always felt this copper-like taste inside my throat that would make me even *more* nauseous...wanted to cry all the time for feeling as if I were boxed into a corner I had no other way out of. The secret that I kept between me and Andrew was so great that it was a wonder I was able to withhold it from my mother without completely losing my shit. But what else was I supposed to do? My mother had been warning me since I got my first period to *never get pregnant* while living under her roof. And the fact that I attended a Catholic high school...nope, no way. Enough said.

The day of the scheduled procedure, Andrew picked me up from school at 3:30 p.m. After I got into his car, he stalled before pulling off from the school's parking lot.

"I think we should look at other options."

My forehead crinkled in confusion, pushing my thick eyebrows towards the middle of my face. "What?"

"I think we should look at other options," he simply said again.

I started to panic, suddenly worried that he wouldn't give me the money for the appointment. I pushed myself up straighter inside the passenger seat and looked over at his innocent face—round, milky brown with kind eyes that hid no wrong. "Andrew, I can't. You *know* I have to do this."

He kept his eyes on mine, however, never raising his voice. "But I talked to a counselor, and she told me that we have other options, that we *don't* have to do this—"

"—*no. I can't.*" I was unmoved, convicted, and I loved him even more for never leaving my side. But I had my mother to contend with, and with or without Andrew's help, it would be *me* who'd have to deal with the repercussions of being unmarried and pregnant, not *him.*

"My mother, Andrew." My tone was suddenly quieted. I turned away and faced the blacktop, not wanting him to see my tears. But he reached over and gently took one of my hands inside his and begged:

"Please, Megan? Can we at least go and just *talk* to her?"

"No. Can we please just *go?*" I remained stone-faced, not allowing myself to feel what he was feeling, to give into my emotions like he was doing because *one of us* had to be strong and focused...because *there was no way* I was going to go home and tell my mother I was expecting. There was just no way.

I ended up telling her, anyway. Three months after I terminated my pregnancy, Andrew and I had already drifted from each other, and I was quickly heading down a dark and lonely tunnel. My grades were crashing, I wanted to throw up every day, especially when I was around crowds—like inside the classroom or on the bus going home. And out of nowhere came the paranoia that everyone was peering at me through this imaginary microscope, judging my every move—from the way I talked to the way I consumed my food during lunch period. One morning during this whole ordeal, I begged my mother to let me stay home from school—something I'd *never* done during any of my years as a student—because I knew once I got there, I'd immediately feel like puking. But she glared at me and calmly replied:

"Whatever you're going through, find a way to get over it. You're going to school."

And when she pulled up to the entrance of Elizabeth Seton

High School 15 minutes later, she surprisingly looked back at me as I got ready to exit the back of her Mustang and asked:

"What is *really* going on with you, Megan? *Huh*? Are you on drugs—?"

"—on *drugs*?"

"Yes, Megan. On drugs."

I drew in a slow breath, my hand on the door's interior handle, and shook my head, feeling as if I had nothing more to lose. "No, Mom. I'm not on *drugs*; I had an *abortion*."

• • •

It was one day in April when my mother had to finally take my bouts of illness seriously. I was spending the fifth morning of that school's quarter in the nurse's office, fighting off the urge to vomit. The nurse called the guidance office and the guidance office then called my mother. My mother ended up leaving work in order to take me to my pediatrician or else, I wouldn't be allowed back in school. When she finally arrived and we were nearing the door to leave, she gave me a look and quietly demanded:

"Let me see the proof that you said you have."

I sighed, careful not to let her hear me, and did as I was told, leaving her in the empty but brightly-lit entrance to go back to the locker room. After five minutes, I returned to Veronica and showed her the receipts from the abortion clinic in Rockville.

She slowly took them in her hands, used a silent moment to finally understand the reason I was quickly dying inside, and handed the papers back to me.

"You make me *sick*."

• • •

I had lost all contact with Andrew by the time I graduated high school in 1998. Since the abortion, I had dreamt several times that our baby would've been a girl. But those dreams ceased a year after that bitter December day. I asked God for forgiveness long before, and was so sure I had also forgiven myself. But on that rare quiet evening, my mind traveled back through all the disastrous relationships I had found myself in after that abortion, and I finally arrived at the year 1997 and to my short, but sweet relationship with Andrew. It was 30 minutes past midnight, but I opened the *Facebook* app on my phone and searched for him. He had such a common first and last name, so several people popped up as suggestions. It took a minute or two to look through profiles, but once my eyes landed on the little girl posed on the pink and gray bicycle, with the same kind eyes I remembered from two decades ago, I knew I had found him.

He looked happy. It didn't seem like he was very active on the site, but from the few pictures he posted, he was married and had one kid—a little girl who resembled every beautiful quality he had from long ago. As I continued to study the girl's eyes, I began to cry. I cried like my heart depended on it, bellowing all of my sorrows and regrets into the stillness of that night. It wasn't for envy that he had moved on with someone else; I was extremely delighted that he had. I broke down into tears that very early morning because I had hurt a man a long time ago—a young man who loved me unselfishly—only to move onto a slew of other young men who would seek to destroy almost every piece of what I had left after I killed that innocent part of me, that December day.

I'm sorry, Andrew.

1

Two Duffel Bags

It's one of the hardest things in the world—learning to reach way down into the pit of your belly to finally discover the self-worth that everyone should come with at birth, when you were never taught that it always existed in the first place. I've made terrible mistakes because I hated myself, never believing I deserved more than what I continuously accepted. Always looking to the next person for my happiness because I never thought *I* was enough.

I was eighteen when I found out I was pregnant again. After I told my father, he purchased a bus ticket for me to travel to D.C. from Austin in order to work things out with the father of my child. I couldn't stay with him anymore since I had fucked up. I understood, though; if just turning eighteen didn't instantly turn me into an official adult, that pregnancy sure as hell did. And my father was under no obligation to continue hosting me under his roof, especially since he had warned me *not* to get pregnant before I traveled back up north in early June.

I had called Adam the day I took the test two weeks before and told him the good news. Well, it *should have been* good news— it was *his* idea that we have a baby in the first place. It had taken us just that one time for me to conceive, my being too stupid to understand that all Adam wanted was to know how good it felt to shoot his baby-making juice outside the constraints of a condom. And then again, maybe deep down I *did* know. But his words I had hung onto, like a drowning person clings onto a life rafter, because that's what I needed at the time.

I want to make a baby with you.

It had been said so gently to me over the phone during one of our many conversations we had since I moved to my father's. My mother had already disowned me by the time she found out about the abortion and I finished high school; her goals for helping me go to college, as was the plan for the last fifteen years, completely vanished when I told her about the abortion my junior year.

"I won't support you in college. You will join the Air Force, and since Basic Training is in San Antonio, you can go live with your father until then."

Art had been my life. That's who I was. That's what I lived and breathed for as long as I could remember. Even with the partial scholarship I received from Moore College of Art & Design in Philadelphia, I would still never be able to redeem myself with Veronica.

I held onto my craft for as long as I could, but when Veronica finally shipped me off to my father, I lost total sense of self, my identity shattered, just like that. By the time I had made it back to Texas, my body was there, but almost everything previously inside it was gone. I no longer smiled, I no longer laughed. Everything— from putting on my clothes in the mornings to brushing my teeth in the evenings—required maximum effort. I was barely consuming 400 calories per day, and during those rare moments I *could* eat, I'd wait until everyone was sleeping to avoid my sudden fear of eating in front of people. I wasn't able to keep a job, either, because being around people still scared the absolute shit out of me like it did after I had the abortion. Sleeping began evading me, too. I ached for the peace that came with it, but every time I drifted, the impending need to vomit would jolt my frail body back awake, a state of being I now dreaded because I didn't know how to continue living with this internal torture.

But Adam had switched up on me the same as Veronica had when she told me I wasn't going to Philadelphia after the summer ended. He didn't share in the excitement of the new baby coming; instead, he told me that he would take care of *the baby*, just not *me*.

"Well, you can come stay with me and my mom." That was Cheyanne, Adam's first cousin. But I wasn't sure I could trust her anymore since *she* was the one who had insisted that I meet her "wonderful cousin" almost three months back, the same man who was now denying he'd ever laid eyes on me. You couldn't tell me that she really *had no clue* her cousin would turn out to be a complete dirt bag.

"I'll pick you up from the bus station, and then you can come stay with me until we figure this thing out." That was Nathan. He was Adam's best friend and Cheyanne's twenty-something boyfriend from the time she had been a sophomore in high school. Even though he had, apparently, just married *someone else* two months prior.

Yeah, I know, it was a weird set-up.

But I didn't have many choices at that point, and I knew my father didn't want me at the house he'd been sharing with his girlfriend, living with them as my choice to keep the pregnancy quickly becoming an eye sore for them. So I agreed to let Nathan pick me up from the Greyhound station when I finally made the nearly two-day bus trip into Washington, D.C.

When I got off at the bus depot, I used a payphone to call Adam. The phone rang only twice before the automated voice on the other end picked up and informed me:

Sorry, but this phone has been temporarily disconnected.

I continued to hold the phone to my ear, hoping that I was only imagining things. His phone *couldn't* be disconnected, not when I'd just spoken to him about my plans for coming back home two days earlier. "Maybe something's just wrong with his line," I muttered quietly. I blew out a frustrated breath, wiped out from the twenty-three-hour long bus trip. After a minute, I hung up and began searching my brain for someone else I could call *other than Nathan* (who, by the way, worked with Adam at the Coast Guard Station). Don't get me wrong— Nathan's heart was always pure and unselfish, but I didn't feel right about relying on him since he was married (as far as I knew).

But I dialed Nathan, anyway, and let him know I had arrived. About an hour later, he happily bounced into the station with Cheyanne on his arm. It was nearing 11 p.m.—where was his *wife...?*

In any event, I was grateful to see both of them. Cheyanne and I had been close since she started at Elizabeth Seton her freshman year, even though she pretty much dictated the whole of our friendship. Much bigger in size than the 98 pounds I had inadvertently slimmed down to by the end of my senior year, I usually deferred to her because she consistently radiated strength and confidence (while also commanding compliance), while my growing anxiety tirelessly rendered me weak and afraid (and submissive).

"Hey preggo...let's get you in the car." She and I embraced and Nathan gave a sympathetic pat on my back. A few moments later we were all seated in his late model Toyota Corolla. As I watched the dark city pass by, I kept quiet as I replayed the automated message Adam had kindly left for me:

Sorry, but this phone has been temporarily disconnected.

10

• • •

I had drifted off, and when I awakened, Cheyanne had already been dropped off at her mom's apartment in Mt. Rainier, a small town situated on the border of D.C. and Maryland. Twenty minutes later, Nathan pulled up to a neighborhood sidewalk and parallel-parked his car. I was confused when I realized we were at Nathan's row house in Northwest.

"I thought I was going to stay in a hotel...?"

"Well, I won't have the money until tomorrow, so you can just stay here in the basement until then."

I sighed almost inaudibly so that he wouldn't hear me. He was nice enough to rescue me, but I was beginning to wish I had never left Texas. Nothing about this seemed good.

He felt my reluctance coming from the backseat of his car and turned back to give me a kind smile. "It's okay, Megan. We'll figure everything out tomorrow."

• • •

Tomorrow was ushered in by the abrupt awakening I received at the very start of dawn. There was a figure standing over my head, shaking my shoulders some, trying to rouse my attention. "Get up... get up!" she whispered loudly. I was scared. My eyes popped open and I was face-to-face with a brown-skinned woman who resembled an older female version of Nathan in the early morning light.

"You've got to go! I'm sorry, but Nathan can't *keep doing things like this*. He has a *wife...she's crazy...*and she'll be home from her shift at McDonald's soon!"

Omigod. I pulled my shit together real quickly, forcing the sleep off. From the way Nathan had always complained about his wife to the way he and Cheyanne always seemed connected by

11

adhesive, I had no idea that his wife was still living with him and his mom. I fiercely rubbed my eyes. "I'm sorry," I told the woman. "I'll leave right now..."

The woman was apologetic. "I'm sorry, too. You seem like a real nice girl, but I can't have you here when Tracy gets home."

And with that, I gathered my two duffel bags and left Nathan's house. Once safely outdoors and on the sidewalk that lined the other row houses, I looked at my watch: 6:45 a.m. I had absolutely *no idea* what to do next. So I began walking.

At about eight o'clock later that morning, I passed a guy who was standing by a car. He asked me if I was okay. I looked at him through the hot morning sun and forced a smile as I slowed my steps. "I'm okay...thanks." I resumed my rhythm.

"You sure? You don't seem like it. What's your name?"

Grateful for the friendly voice, I stopped and turned towards him. "It's Megan."

"Megan. Hmm...are you alright?"

I let out a breath, set my two duffel bags onto the sidewalk and wiped the water from my brow. "Actually, no. I don't have any-where to go right now." Such a stupid thing to say to a stranger, but I had no idea where I was going next. Didn't even have a cell phone to call anybody, even *if* I had anybody to call.

"Well, you can come to my house. I'll fix you something to eat. Then, you can make a few phone calls if you need to."

My smile was apprehensive as I studied his appearance. He looked to be in his mid-twenties, tall, gangly, dark brown skin. He opened his car door for me. And like a willing victim, I stepped in.

He (I never got his name) took me to his apartment, which was in the small but bustling city of Silver Spring, Maryland, just outside of Northwest D.C. Actually, it wasn't his place—it was *his aunt's*, who surprisingly never emerged from her room the whole time I was there. He fixed me White Castle cheeseburgers and poured me orange juice. We didn't talk much. Just sat around and watched TV in the living room. The whole time, I tried to come up with my next move. I thought about calling my father, but didn't even know what I would tell him. Definitely didn't want to call Nathan *ever again*. I was pissed that he had left me at his house to fend for myself against crazy-ass *Tracy*, never having the foresight to tell me that he wasn't going to be there the next day. Even though he was a good person, he sometimes neglected to think things through (like I had any room to say that). And I definitely wasn't going to call Cheyanne (who I secretly blamed for pushing me into this mess with her fucked up cousin).

Sorry, but this line has been temporarily disconnected.

Around 8 p.m., the guy finally stood from the sofa we'd been sharing and instructed me to follow him. I walked behind him into a bedroom and watched him close the door behind me. He motioned for me to sit down on his bed before proceeding to rummage through a bag of VHS videos. After about a minute, he pulled out a movie and showed it to me.

"Do you watch stuff like this?"

I narrowed my eyes and studied the front of the movie. It was a porn flick. I was floored, but tried my best to keep my disgust hidden. I put up my hand. "Um, no. I don't watch those at all."

He stared at me for a second, watching me hard with his dark brown eyes, which were quickly transforming into something evil. "Well, we're gonna watch it, anyway."

I tore my eyes from his and looked down at the dirty carpet. I gave a small nod of my head.

He put in his tape. I refused to look at the TV screen. Shortly, the offensive sounds of *oohs* and *aahs* and *splish-splashing* began filling the tiny room. I couldn't believe he was watching this shit with his aunt in the next room.

And every minute or so, he would turn his gaze from the TV screen and fix it onto my body. My heart began to pound through my chest, and before I knew it, he had turned his body from the porn and placed his long, bony fingers on my legs. When he began to reach for the button on my shorts, I immediately shoved his hand away.

"No," I objected quietly. "I'm pregnant...."

He was taken aback. He moved his hand away and his face became scary. "Then, *bitch*, what the fuck you come over here for?"

I blinked, my naivete leaving me shocked. I quickly gathered myself together and stood.

He stood as well and took a step towards me, coming within an inch of my face. "Get the fuck out my house then, *bitch*!"

I reached to open the closed door with a hand that wouldn't stop shaking, wondering how the hell he could behave like this in his aunt's house. And *where was his aunt*? She couldn't hear all the shit going on outside her room...??

I quickly made my way to the living room and grabbed my belongings, tears beginning to blind my eyes as I rushed to invent my next move. The guy was almost on my ass by the time I opened the front door to the apartment, and I briefly wondered if he was going to try pull me back in so he could rape me.

"Yeah, hurry up and get your shit and get the fuck outta here!" His mouth was now next to my ear and his voice made my eardrum vibrate painfully.

Fleeing down the steps that led to his third floor apartment, I prayed through short bursts of air that he wouldn't follow me. He didn't. Instead, he shouted:

"*Bitch*, I hope your stupid ass gets raped and killed out there!!"

Once I finally reached the last step of the apartment complex and met the nighttime sky, I darted for the other side of the street. Glancing behind me to make sure the guy was long gone, I stopped to analyze my location. I was out of breath and my insides began cramping.

The world seemed deserted, but there were several street lights ensuring my safety. Less than a quarter mile up the street from me was a shopping center. There was a Giant grocery store, a Hallmark card store, a Dress Barn, a gas station, and a couple of eateries. I began sprinting the sidewalk—heart beating through my chest, duffel bags banging against my widening hips—hoping to find a payphone nearby.

Coming up to the center, I was surprised to realize that I was only a mere ten minutes away from the townhouse Adam shared with his mother. My heart beat even faster. Hopefully there would be a payphone...and hopefully my last option would work.

I entered the empty plaza and walked carefully through the few cars scattered here and there. I spotted a payphone near a Chevy Chase Bank and crossed my fingers. Looking around me first to make sure there was nobody lurking around the ATM machine, I took out two quarters and dialed his number.

I took a quick look at my watch in the dim light as I listened to the soft ringing. It was nearing 11 p.m. "Hello?" Adam answered sleepily on the third ring. I licked my dehydrated lips. My heart's vibrations reached the inside of my ears.

"Um...Adam...it's Megan." I waited for him to reply. He didn't. So I spoke nervously, but quickly. "Um...I'm out here, not too far from you, and I don't have anywhere to go. Can you please come get me?"

He didn't reply at first. *Please, God, help me*, I prayed silently. Adam's silence frightened every filament, nerve cell, and bone inside of me, and I hated every moment that was my life right then.

I bit down hard on my lips and waited for his reply, holding the black phone against my ear as tightly as I could manage while tasting traces of blood that were beginning to fill the stillness.

He finally spoke. "I'm in bed and I have work tomorrow. What do you want *me* to do about it?" His voice was robotic and unfeeling. I blinked my eyes in disbelief as I continued to grip the earpiece with all my might, praying that he would speak again... that he would tell me that he was just kidding...and ask me where he should come get me. But he didn't. I must have held onto that phone for a good forty-five seconds, praying hard to hear a miracle that would never come.

Shameful tears began dripping from my eyes. "Um...ok. Well... thank you." And with that, I hung up the phone. I remained by it for a few minutes, however, hoping he would call it back. He just *had* to look at his caller ID, see the number, and ring it right back. I was pregnant with his baby and *just had to believe* he wouldn't leave me stranded.

The phone never rang.

Thankfully, there was a park bench a few feet from the ATM. I rested my two duffel bags on it and sat down. I cried out into the quiet night air and begged God to tell me what to do next. Ten minutes after sobbing, a car pulled up next to the ATM. A young woman about twenty-two or twenty-three stepped out and made a move for the ATM when she suddenly noticed me on the bench.

"Oh my God! You scared me! Are you okay?"

I burst into more tears. "No, I'm not." My voice was shaky and I must have sounded like I was a twelve-year-old all over again. "I'm pregnant, and I just called my boyfriend, and he refuses to come get me. I have...I have really nowhere else to go. And I don't know what to do..."

The girl came over to where I sat and wrapped her arms around me. "Oh my God. I'm so sorry! Here, get in the car and you can come home with me."

Her unexpected kindness stopped the flow of tears immediately. "No, you don't have to do this...you don't even know me..."

She smiled at me. "It's really okay. My conscience won't allow me to leave you out here like this." She turned back towards the ATM and withdrew some cash before carefully placing my bags into the backseat of her Rav 4. We traveled together to her house in Rockville, about twenty-five minutes north.

My angel's name was Allison, and she welcomed me into her townhome with ease. She let me shower, gave me a change of clothes, and made me a grilled cheese sandwich with tomato soup. She then let me sleep in the same bed with her...and her eight, healthy, fat cats. I'd never been an animal person, but enjoyed the comfort and the warmth they wrapped me in while I slept. In the middle of the night, I even awakened to one of the cats, curled on top of the pillow that my head rested on. God, I wished I could feel that peace forever.

Anxiety riddled my insides the next morning. The plan was for Allison to take me to lunch and then drop me off at Union Station. During my bus trip to D.C. I had met a girl my age who told me that I could always get help from her if I needed it. She had given me her number and told me that I could call at any time. I didn't want to rely on her, but I was so desperate and knew I couldn't call Nathan *ever again* for help. I was still recovering from the moment his mother had rushed me out of her home.

Allison treated me to a nice lunch that included a club sandwich, fries and a Pepsi at her dad's deli in Annapolis. After that, it was time for me to get back on my journey.

We said good-bye at Union Station and she kissed my cheek for good luck. I'd never been treated so nicely by a stranger before in all of my life. To this day, I pray that God blesses her for coming to my rescue that night.

I entered the waiting area where people were standing by for their arriving trains. The Amtrak was heading to cities such as Philadelphia and New York. I made my way to the set of payphones on the wall and pulled Rae's number out of my pants pocket. She was a young woman, about my age, who had hopped on the Greyhound bus during its stop in Tennessee. She was headed my way, as well, and we had nearly fourteen hours to bond over the friends she was eager to see in the District, and my shitty-ass circumstances. She had sympathetically given me her number in case I needed a friend while in D.C.

Ring, ring, ring. Someone finally picked up, but informed me that Rae was not home. I hung up the stupid phone. Here we go again. My heart began pounding and I searched behind me for a seat to sit down in and ponder my next step. I started watching the black board that displayed all the departing/arriving trains. Every few minutes or so, the letters and numbers would change as they continuously offered updated information on times and train numbers. My eyes were tired. Holding my two duffel bags close to me, I closed my eyes for a few and prayed for a miracle.

I opened my eyes when I felt some fluid trickling from the inside of me. I checked the watch on my wrist: 7:30 p.m. It had been ten minutes to five when I had decided to rest for just a few. I quickly sat up in my chair, checking to the right of me to make sure my bags were still there. I wiped my eyes, regaining my focus. God, people who saw me sleeping there must have thought I was some kind of vagrant or something. I was embarrassed and my cheeks began flushing something hot. I looked for signs for the nearest restroom. Once spotted, I got up and rushed to the toilet.

Inside the small stall, I saw nothing but bright red blood

smeared all over my undergarments and upper thighs. The room started to spin, and those damn tears that seemed to come from an endless supply inside of me began to blind my eyes as the panic set in immediately.

I cleaned myself up as best I could and called Cheyanne from the same payphone I had used to call the girl I met on the bus.

"Hello, Cheyanne?"

"Yeah...Megan?"

"Yeah, it's me," I almost cried into the phone. I took some breaths, trying my best to hold it all together in front of all the happy trip-takers inside of Union Station. "I'm bleeding everywhere and I don't know what to do."

"Call 911, Megan. Get off the phone with me and call 911. Then, call me back."

She seemed concerned. I was grateful for that. I hung up with her and did as I was told. Not wanting to sit down and risk smearing the seat with my blood, I remained by the phone, feverish with mortification, and waited for the ambulance as the dizziness evolved into nausea, forcing me to slowly breathe back the bile so I wouldn't further humiliate myself inside Union Station.

2

No Tears

When I was ten, I told my diary that I had thoughts of killing myself. That would be my first time contemplating suicide. Gerald, my mother's boyfriend of a few years after her divorce from my father, "found" the small pink and white journal with the purple lined pages one afternoon while I was at school. In his usual custom of shaming me, he shared with my mother what he'd discovered later that evening.

"So you want to kill yourself...?" Veronica asked me while the three of us remained at the dining table after dinner was finished.

I blinked a few times as I began to feel the heavy tears automatically begin to blind my eyes. That shit was private, and the sneer my mother held on her face, plus the satisfied look Gerald wore as he awaited my answer made me wish I had slit my wrists when I had *first* confided in my diary two weeks before.

Stunned, all I could do was watch the two of them in painful silence. But I didn't want to show my embarrassment, so I bowed my head.

"Look at me," Veronica calmly demanded.

I snapped my head back to attention, my tears having no choice but to slip over the brims of my lids. I watched my mother as she took a sip of her red wine before carefully replacing the glass onto the oak tabletop. She then lowered her neck in order to bring her face closer to mine, her deliberate contortions reminding me of a vulture's before she dives into her feast. Her glassy eyes remained fixed onto mine as Gerald continued to look on from the opposite side of the table, his arms crossed against his chest as he enjoyed my torment. My cries to my mother about the way Gerald treated me went unheard. Whenever I got into his version of "trouble," he'd dole out corporal punishment like I was a man; when my mother wasn't around and I had done a stellar job with my chores, he'd make me kiss him in his filthy lips like I was a consenting adult. Sometimes, I'd plead with my father over long-distance phone calls to rescue me from Maryland and bring me back to the safety that the little house in the quiet Texas cul-de-sac had provided before my parents split. But there was something about a custody agreement he had to uphold with my mother...

After a moment, Veronica finally separated her perfectly painted lips and spoke softly...but deliberately:

When you finally decide to kill yourself, make sure you cut your wrists vertically instead of horizontally...and do it over the bathtub so that you won't make a mess.

• • •

Hot tears stung my eyes as Adam's words from the previous night continued to singe a hole through my core. *I'm in bed and I have work tomorrow—what do you want me to do about it?* After nearly begging him to come rescue me the other night, his flat tone had both shocked and embarrassed me. Wiping the water from my eyes, I continued to gaze up at the ceiling of my hospital room.

Three hours earlier, I arrived at Howard University Hospital, a few ambulance minutes away from Union Station. Once the doctors examined me for the cause of the bleeding, it was finally determined that my body was trying to miscarry; however, the embryo's heartbeat was still alive and stable. They termed it a *threatened miscarriage.*

"If you don't have any family or support from the father of the child, why don't you think about having an abortion? You know, it's not too late. You're only about seven weeks."

That was my nurse from an hour ago. My eyes rolled to the left as I forced myself to look at the woman. Was she serious? I wanted to shoot her a hateful look, tell her to go fuck herself. But I was 18 and scared, and there was nobody else there in that lonely hospital room with me. What she offered made total sense.

"Okay," I told her in my usual gutless voice. "Thank you."

She tried to redeem herself by mustering a sympathetic smile with her thin, aged lips before giving me a slight pat on my shoulder, probably realizing that she had stepped out of line by playing counselor. "Well, get some rest. Tomorrow morning, we'll probably discharge you."

I was grateful for the safe place to sleep, but couldn't keep my eyes closed as I tossed and turned all night. My heart tried to pump its way through my chest walls as my mind worked furiously to figure out what I was going to do the next day. I thought about Veronica and wondered very briefly if she would let me come back home if I told her I had nowhere else to go. But I almost laughed out loud inside of the eerie silence of that hospital room, knowing better than anything that my mother would rather amputate her own leg *on her own* than have the humiliation of a pregnant, unwed daughter anywhere near her.

I was discharged at 10 a.m. the next day. They gave me my walking papers that instructed: *Threatened Miscarriage...*

Modified Bed Rest for the Next 24 Hours...No Strenuous Exercise... No Sex for the next 72 Hours...No Carrying Anything Over Ten Pounds...

I smirked at the last order. My luggage alone must have weighed 25 pounds easily. My heart began racing again, and I briefly wondered why I had chosen life over death the night Veronica and Gerald had made a mockery of my desire to die.

I gathered my things together and headed downstairs to the outside world. Before I exited, I set my bags onto the tiled floor and picked up the payphone. Dialing my father's house collect, I prayed he would accept the call.

I anxiously waited while the operator connected us. "Hello?" My father answered on the third ring. His voice was low and cautious. I clenched the coiled telephone wire as I tried to come up with something effective to say.

"You have a collect call from Megan," the automated voice announced. "Will you accept the charges?"

I held my breath and waited, praying that my father would say yes, but understanding that secretly, he didn't want the responsibility of bailing me out.

A few seconds later, I heard him say, "Hello...Megan?" I slowly let out all of the air from my body and began talking.

"Hello...Dad? It's me. I just got out of the hospital—"

"—you did? What happened?"

I spoke nervously and breathlessly, knowing that it was a long shot to call my father for help. "I almost miscarried the baby...but it's okay now...they just told me that I shouldn't be walking around too much or carrying heavy loads with me..." I swallowed thickly and waited, worried that this call was a waste of my father's time.

After half a minute passed, he told me, "Well, Megan...just

make sure you are more careful...and try not to carry too many heavy things with you."

Whatever life that still remained inside of me was let out in a defeated but quiet exhalation. I didn't want my father to realize I was actually reaching out to him for help...because I didn't want to admit that I had messed up...that things were only getting worse and that I still had no place to rest my tired body. That I couldn't continue keeping up the facade that the father of my kid still wanted me—wanted *us*—and that I was actually as dumb as everyone said I was for even believing that he had in the first place.

"Ok, Dad. Thanks. I'll keep in touch."

"Ok, sweetie. Keep me posted."

I looked up towards the stark white ceiling of the hospital and silently cursed. Things in the hospital were swiftly picking up as doctors, nurses, and patients hustled and bustled around me. Happy people. People who had families who gave a shit. I tried to maintain my composure because I didn't want to show the worry on my face.

I hung up the phone.

• • •

I found myself by Georgia Avenue of Northwest D.C. when I finally left the temporary shelter the hospital had provided me. Instantly, I shielded my eyes from the hot August sun that nearly blinded me with her promising light. There was a McDonald's across the street so I decided to use the little bit of money I had in order to feed myself so that I wouldn't starve my poor child to death.

I sat down with my Value Meal for as long as I could without giving away the fact that I had no place else to go. The chicken sandwich and fries tasted so good going down, and I prayed that the leftover $20 I had in my wallet would last until I figured out what to do next.

An hour later, I decided it was doing me no good to keep sitting at McDonald's, so I dumped my trash, only carrying my half-filled cup of sweet tea and my duffel bags. After standing on Florida Avenue for what seemed like an eternity, I crossed the busy street and headed for the Exxon gas station. Maybe on my way over there, I would think of someone else I could phone for help.

But of course, no luck. It was nearing 12 p.m., and I was feeling more and more stupid as I lingered at the gas pumps, gazing at the Exxon sign, as if it would magically give me the answer I'd been praying for. The tips of my ears burned with shame and I finally decided to sit down on the sidewalk that ran parallel to the station. My bags next to me, I propped my elbow onto my knee, and rested my chin inside my hand.

Looking down at the white ID band the hospital had adorned me with, I mentally ran through all my options (as if I had any). I suddenly straightened my posture as a thought appeared: *I could head back to Texas, get rid of the pregnancy like my father originally suggested, and then I'd have a place to live again.* Problem solved.

I'm in bed and I have work tomorrow...what do you want me to do about it?

I shuddered inside the early afternoon heat, involuntarily replaying Adam's cold words from two nights ago. Those words would haunt me for the next eighteen years.

• • •

"Um, miss...are you alright?"

I jumped at the voice and turned my head towards the sound. I didn't realize there was someone standing so close to me.

26

The voice asked me again: "I'm sorry, I don't mean to startle you, but I was just seeing if you were okay...?"

I shielded my eyes from the sun and looked up towards the man. He was tall, slightly built, had dark skin, and his accent was from the Caribbean. I remained seated and let out a slightly annoyed breath. He was nice enough to ask, but I was tired of repeating the same pathetic story like it was going to miraculously open worlds for me if I told it to the right person.

"I'm pregnant and I have nowhere to go." I lifted my left arm up for him to see the hospital wristband. "I just got out of the hospital and I don't know what to do next. So I came here to think of *something*." I let down my hand and looked back towards the ground, sighing once more, feeling as if I had nothing else left to lose.

"So where are your parents?"

His voice was deep, but kind. "My mother and I don't speak anymore, and my father's in Texas. He sent me up here so that I can work things out with the father of my child, but as you can see"—I smirked out loud—"that's not working out so well."

Out of the corner of my eye, I saw him shift from his left to his right foot, clearly uncomfortable with my sense of humor.

"So you have contact with your father still?"

I gave a casual shrug of my shoulders, keeping my gaze downward. "I guess you could call it that. I spoke to him when I left the hospital this morning, but there wasn't much he could say." My conscience began reminding me of how childlike I really was. How the hell did I get myself into this *stupid* situation? And now, I was sitting there, on the stoop of a dirty-ass gas station, telling *another* stranger about my shitty-ass problems.

I heard the man change his position once again before he fell silent for a moment. I continued to look down, suddenly wondering if Adam had thought about me since my S.O.S. call from two nights ago.

"Tell you what," the man finally spoke. "Give me your father's number, and I'm going to call him..."

I quickly raised my head in objection. "No. There's no point. I've gotta figure this out on my own, sir."

He raised his index finger in opposition. "But, young lady, a father would *never* want his daughter out here on the streets like this if he knew. I have three daughters of my own, and I *have* to believe that your father has a heart."

His accent came from Trinidad, I was sure. I had to give him a small smile—he offered me a little bit of hope. I let him have the number to my dad's house and waited as he stepped inside his dark SUV to make the call.

Ten minutes later, the stranger returned to me with a satisfied look on his face. "See, I told you, your father would *have to* understand the predicament his daughter is in..."

I raised my eyebrows at this, but continued to listen. He saw my expression and gave a half-smile. "C'mon! I know it seems like a terrible thing right now, but believe me, it *will* get better..."

I shook my head at this.

He watched me and waited for a better reply, and when he realized he wasn't going to get one, he continued:

Well, young lady, your father wants you to call him later this evening. He is purchasing you a ticket right now, and when you call him later on, he'll have the confirmation number so that you can hop on the train and head back to Austin tomorrow morning.

• • •

After securing a room for me at the Budget Inn on New York Avenue, only three miles from the Exxon, the second saint who came to my rescue in less than forty-eight hours, gave me fifty dollars so that I could order delivery, buy a prepaid calling card to call my father that evening, and pay for a taxi to run me to the train station in the morning. After that, he wished me well, and continued on his way. That was the last I saw or heard from him. He never offered me his number or his last name because he was married and didn't want any trouble. He helped me during one of my greatest times of need, expecting nothing in return.

I ordered Chinese that night and once settled, I reluctantly called my father. As expected, he didn't have much to say, but let me know there'd be a ticket waiting for me at Union Station, departing at 8 a.m. the next morning. Closing my eyes, I banged my head lightly against the thin headboard several times, feeling guilty that I had made myself such a burden for him.

Minutes passed and I realized just how quiet it was inside of the worn motel room. I picked up the telephone again and used the calling card to reach Adam at his job, where he couldn't escape me. I knew the calling card wasn't for that purpose, but I just had to try one more time...

"Coast Guard Station Annapolis. Fireman Hartley speaking."

His voice made me feel like melting. I felt so lucky that he was the one to answer the phone, and immediately forgot about his leaving me out in the late night hours to fend for myself, less than two days ago. My heart fluttered inside my chest, and I was at a loss for words. I mean, *what do you say* to the man who got you pregnant and now refused to acknowledge he ever knew you?

He spoke again. "Coast Guard Station Annapolis..."

I found my voice. God, I was such a dunce! "Uh, hey, it's Megan."

It took him a couple of seconds. I licked my dry lips as I waited nervously.

"Hey." He spoke softly. Not with the cold voice he used when I asked him for help the other night.

You're an idiot, Megan! He has to keep his tone down because he's at work!

I ignored the smart part of me that still existed, just glad to hear his voice. "Hey," I said back to him. "I just got out of the hospital..." I waited to see if he was interested in hearing more.

"What happened? Are you okay?"

He almost sounded concerned. My heart moved happily once again. *God, I loved this man.* "Well, I almost had a miscarriage. I wound up bleeding everywhere. Had to be taken to the emergency room..."

"Everything okay?" He still kept his voice low, and still managed to sound worried. I was turning into a puddle quickly.

"Yeah, I just have to stay off my feet for a while. Ummm...I'm going back to Texas in the morning. For the night, I'm staying at the Budget Inn." I let him know my location, just in case he decided to join me in my hotel room for the night...

He seemed to think for a moment. Then he cleared his throat. "Well, I have to get back to this job. Just, um...just call me when you get back home tomorrow, okay?"

My heart halted her girlish dance and plummeted into the deepest part of my stomach. I immediately realized how stupid and desperate I sounded, and my face began to flush something hot. *Told you, you stupid bitch,* my conscience hissed at me. Tears surfaced from my belly to my eyes, but just so I would appear as if that short conversation had no effect on me at all, I simply stated:

Okay, I'll call you soon. Take care.

I hung up the phone.

4

835 South Trinity Street

His lips formed the perfect *O* as I descended the long staircase, slowly and cautiously, the silky material of the white dress gently enveloping my developing curves. With each step I took, the older wooden steps creaked lightly, the only sound in the otherwise quiet house as his eyes locked onto mine for the very first time. When I made it to the last step, he slowly rose from his seat.

My face blushed and my eyes skittered to and fro in an effort to replace their focus on the giant plant that rested next to the armchair he was just seated in. Cheyanne immediately took control of the situation, though, making a very noticeable noise with her throat, as if attempting to clear it.

"Chica, this is my cousin Adam. And Adam, this—" Cheyanne made a dramatic gesture towards me with her hand (complete with a wicked grin on her round face)— "as you know, is Megan."

Adam kept his gaze on me from ten feet away as he continued to stand by the armchair. My face heated again as I noticed the gentle way he watched my eyes with an amazement that seemed to radiate from within. Finally, he made a move forward, covering the distance between us with slow, deliberate steps. He offered me his hand.

"Um, hi. I'm Adam. It's a pleasure to finally see you in person." His sandy brown face broke into a smile, revealing two perfect rows of white teeth.

My face burned again from his attention, and I was sure that its burnt peanut butter brown was quickly morphing into a deep rose. As Adam held my gaze, the world seemed to pause on its axis, for just a moment, as we became acquainted with one another through just the touch of our hands. I nervously but excitedly studied the man in front of me, pleasantly surprised that Cheyanne did not disappoint by bringing him to the house, even though I had originally objected. Adam was average height, standing about two inches taller than my 5'2" frame. He was of a thin, but muscular build; the color of his skin reminded me of the sand that covered the beaches on South Padre Island. And the slight slant of his gentle but piercing light brown eyes showed that he was not only of African-American descent, but also of some Asian heritage from generations past...

"Where are you from?" I heard myself unexpectedly ask.

He let go of my hand and crossed his arms over his chest. He wore a navy blue T-shirt that read *United States Coast Guard*, and I made a mental note that the blue against his skin created the most beautiful contrast.

He kept his eyes on me when he spoke, shifting his balance between his feet. "Well, my mother is black, and my father's mother is a mix of Chinese and Japanese. What about you?"

I smiled, pleased that he was interested. "I was born in Spain, but came to the states when I was about three."

"Really?" He uncrossed his arms and put his hands in his jeans pockets, tilting his head slightly upward. "Very interesting. You speak Spanish—?"

"—I do."

He moved his feet once more, relaxing his stance a little as he seemed to give my answer some thought. He gave me another delighted smile. "Wow. That's pretty amazing."

My smile spread even wider, threatening to break my face.

"Well, if you two are done with all the particulars, could we *please* get something to eat? I'm fucking starving!"

That was Vanessa, another classmate of mine, who would be graduating with me come the next afternoon. The world resumed its rotation once again, and Adam and I tore our eyes from one another and looked towards the top of the staircase. Vanessa stood, tall and lean and goddess-like, her naturally curly locks falling over her shoulders as she looked down upon the rest of us. She feigned impatience and playfully rolled her dark eyes at us. She then set her attention onto Adam.

"Adam, do you like how perfectly I made her up?" I watched Vanessa purse her lips, constrict her eyes, and hold her index finger up before twirling it in the air. "Megan, do a quick spin so everyone can see my handiwork."

"Omigod, Vanessa," I quietly muttered, but did as I was told, quickly turning my face downwards as I felt another smile begin to form. I turned carefully on my bare toes so that Adam, Vanessa, and Cheyanne could get a good look at the dress I chose for my graduation ceremony. The dress was pure white, slim, and clung onto my thin frame from two spaghetti straps. It was a simple garment, but the two slits on either side that ran from the floor to my knees added a subtle sexiness to it.

"One more turn, chica!"

That was Cheyanne again, enjoying the show. Before I made another pirouette, I gave her a friendly glower, my internal temperature rising as I felt Adam's eyes glued onto me. My freshly-done curls, courtesy of Vanessa, whirled with me inside of the sun-lit living room of Vanessa's parents' D.C. row house, and...I was happy.

• • •

"Megan. We're here. Wake up."

I opened my eyes. Happiness nowadays didn't seem to last but for a few moments for me. I wasn't asleep—just had my eyes closed for the car ride as my heart ached for better times. My father's voice was stern, something I wasn't used to. I was quickly realizing how much disdain I had brought to him and his new family because of the foolish decision I made in believing that Adam wanted to make a family of our own with me.

Yes, it must have sounded like the most outlandish idea in the world, when Adam told me over the phone, some 1500 miles away in Maryland, that he wanted me to have his baby. Of course it sounded silly to the average person that, after knowing me for less than three months, he actually wanted a kid with me. But I wasn't the average person—I was eighteen, full of hopes and dreams and dangerous innocence...and a severely shattered mind because I couldn't bear my mother's rejection of me any longer. I graduated high school depressed and hopeless, and couldn't be alone with my own immobilizing, invisible demons. By the time I met Adam, I believed I was actually sick because of all the throwing up my body constantly demanded I do. My mind was so gone I had also developed an addiction to antacids shortly after terminating my pregnancy. Until my "sickness" was diagnosed as General Anxiety Disorder, you could never catch me without a bottle of water and a roll of Tums tucked secretly inside my palm—*never*. My dependency on the chalky pills was so bad, the doctor who performed my endoscopy in Texas warned me of the calcifications inside my kidneys that were starting to form because of the calcium overload I had been indulging in.

I saw no sense in living since I was forced to build a new life in a state I had long ago abandoned when my mother left my father. Adam was the only purpose I had for living. All I wanted was to belong to someone who would accept me and keep me safe. And why *not* Adam? During our very brief time together while I was still living in Maryland—before Veronica shipped me off to my dad's—we fell in love. He treated me *like* he loved me. Though only for a moment, I was allowed to live outside of my head and finally *enjoy* life. I was stupidly happy, and he was the only person who could make it happen.

. . .

It was a little after 11 p.m. when I followed my father into the quaint ranch house. I was able to quietly meander my way through the large open kitchen and make a sandwich, being careful not to wake up Tamron and her daughter. My dad met Tamron four or five years ago. She had been a recent divorcee, living in Chicago, when she was finally able to whisk my father off his much older feet. But I guess that's what happens when parents divorce, Mom moves light years away, and because of this, the kids get to visit their dad for only two- and- half months out of the calendar year.

Maybe I was a bit biased. Maybe it was the pregnancy hormones. But my mother disliked my father's new lady because she believed Tamron was trying with all her might to displace me and my sister Avery from our place in our father's life. And maybe, Veronica actually had a point...

. . .

When I finished eating, I took a much-needed shower and went to bed in the guest bedroom. Before retiring to his room earlier, my father had mumbled something about making sure I got some rest because we had a trip to make early in the morning.

A trip to finding a job or a trip to the social services building that Tamron had suggested I make when I found out I was pregnant—these were *way* better than the disastrous trip I had taken to D.C., just to plead with a practical ghost to remember his part in creating the life that rested inside of me. I felt strange being back at my dad's house, though, as if I no longer belonged there. But I was so grateful to have a safe roof over my head again that I didn't bother to entertain whether I had any business being back there.

I was up by 9 a.m. the next morning. I dressed and met my father, Tamron, and Tamron's daughter Aja at the dining room table for breakfast.

"When you're done, Megan, I need you to pack your clothes and anything important you'll want to take with you."

That was my father. I paused mid-way, my fork still holding the piece of syrupy pancake towards my mouth. "Everything like *what?*" I watched suspiciously as my father quietly placed his own fork down onto his plate and folded his dark brown hands over his food. He looked at me with a grave face.

"I'm taking you to San Antonio to stay with other pregnant woman like you..."

Pregnant women like me? My heart dropped. "You're *what?*" The question tumbled out of my mouth accidentally, as I didn't want to show my father any disrespect.

My father's head turned to his right some ten degrees and he lowered his eyes. He seemed to struggle some, and I briefly wondered if his decision had anything to do with his relationship with Tamron.

He spoke slowly. "Well, *daughter*, since you were not able to make things work with the father of your child, and your mother is not going to take you back in—"

"—you told *Mom*?" I blurted out angrily.

"Well, I had no choice. You *are* still her daughter."

From the corner of my eye, I saw Aja begin to fidget inside of her high chair. Tamron proceeded to take the last bite of her food before getting up to take her daughter from the table. My father continued after it was just me and him left.

"This is a group home for pregnant girls who have nowhere else to stay. They will take care of you and make sure you get everything necessary for you and your pregnancy. It's in San Antonio, and I'm supposed to have you there by one o'clock today."

I kept my eyes on my father for one whole minute, waiting for him to tell me that he was just telling a really bad joke. When I realized he wasn't, I slowly lowered my fork, having lost all interest in my breakfast.

• • •

There wasn't much to pack. I had been losing pieces of who I once was by the time I had left my mother's house before my graduation, to temporarily take up residence with Vanessa in D.C., to finally move back in with my father in Texas. The only belongings I had left were a few summer outfits, two pairs of shoes, toiletries, my acrylic paints, pastels, and sketchbook, and two small, blank canvases... plus the collection of ten or so photographs that Adam and I had taken together during the very beginning of that summer.

Before leaving my father's house for the last time, I found a pair of scissors and slashed through all those pictures, dropping the shredded remnants of the recent past into a wastebasket.

• • •

I'm in bed, and I have work tomorrow...what do you want me to do about it?

Adam's frigid words to me less than one week ago in the middle of the night echoed inside my head as I watched the outside world silently drift away from the backseat of my father's sedan.

Two hours after we began our trek at 11 that morning, my father entered an older neighborhood on the east side of San Antonio. After a couple of turns through the shabby but quiet roads, he stalled his car just short of an older white house that looked as if it were about two to three stories high. A short metal fence surrounded its perimeter, and the few tufts of green grass that were scattered throughout seemed to struggle to stay alive among the weeds that took over the yard. A wooden sign that had seen better days moved with the slight wind from its metal post that was anchored into the ground next to the sidewalk. When I read the words that were painted in black, my heart began to thud, threatening to free herself from my chest wall and the decrepit neighborhood as my father effortlessly parallel-parked his car on the same side of the street as the rickety old house.

Guadalupe Home
835 South Trinity Street

The year was 1998, and until that moment, I *had no idea* maternity homes still existed in the United States. The tears I had successfully kept inside of my throat during the drive to San Antonio climbed through my insides and made their way to the fronts of my eyes. But I was *not going to cry* in front of my father or Tamron. Instead, I obediently stepped out of the vehicle, traveled towards the back of the car, gathered my few items, and followed my father and his girlfriend to the front door of *The Guadalupe Home.*

4

Good Mothers

Named for *Nuestra Señora de Guadalupe,* or Our Lady of Guadalupe—the Mexican name for the Virgin Mary who appeared before Juan Diego four centuries ago in Mexico City—*The Guadalupe Home* was established as a sanctuary for pregnant women. From youthful teenagers as young as 13, to older women who were dangerously close to running out of healthy eggs for procreation, the home served to help *people like me* get back on their feet. Some women already had children from previous relationships/marriages they had to leave behind; some were already living on the streets and kicking drug habits when they found out they were expecting; one or two others had a history of child abuse/child neglect, and were just sadly waiting for the state of Texas to take their newborns away as soon as the babes took their first breath of air inside the delivery room.

It was a sad state of affairs. There was one young woman by the name of Sandra, a full-blooded Mexican, who moved into the home six months after I had been there. It was one afternoon inside the worn but sun-filled day room, and us girls were sitting around in a circle, genuinely amused by the portable heartbeat monitor that a prenatal nurse came by to show us. As she placed the probe on each one of our bellies, we all got a kick out of hearing evidence of the lives incubating inside of us. But when she came upon Sandra's enormous *vientre* (made huge by the triplets she was carrying, as told to us by Sandra), there were no heartbeats.

Our visiting nurse looked perplexed. "Hmph...that's strange..." The room grew suddenly quiet as Rachel visually inspected her black monitor—turning it off, turning it back on, and tapping the transducer with her index finger.

She looked at Sandra's swollen face and said, "You sure you're having *three* babies?"

Sandra emphatically nodded, her jet black hair swinging with each bob of her head. "Mmm...hmmm...I sure am!"

"Hmmm. Okay, well let me try this again." Nurse Rachel placed the transducer on Sandra's tan belly once again and listened as ten curious eyes, mine included, peered intently as Sandra searched for any signs of life...crickets.

"That's really strange." Rachel removed her device and wiped it off with a small alcohol pad. She gave a nervous chuckle. "You know, sometimes it can be hard to hear a heartbeat when there are so many of them. She chuckled once more. "I'm sure everything is okay, though."

My eyebrows rose.

Turned out, two months later—a few days after I had given birth to my sweet baby boy, Caleb—our night house mother, Janet, began furiously shaking me from my sleep sometime around 1 a.m. one night. I sat straight up as she whispered frantically:

"Megan, Megan—she took my car! She took my keys and now my car is gone!"

"What?" I rubbed the sleep from my eyes and glanced to my right at Caleb, who was still sleeping inside his crib. "*Who* took your car, Janet?"

"Sandra!"

"*Sandra?*"

"Yes! I had fallen asleep on the sofa, and all of a sudden, I heard the front door slam shut and I woke up. Next thing I know, I'm looking for my keys, which I had next to me, and they were gone! I run outside, and I see her and a man pulling off with my car!"

I threw off the covers, finally awake enough to understand what Janet was saying to me. "Are you sure?"

She nodded her head quickly and through the dark of my tiny room, I could see tears trailing from her eyes.

"Come on, let's go."

We hurried to the staircase and crept downstairs, careful not to wake the other women. I made my way to the old-fashioned kitchen and carefully opened the door leading to the back of the home, the sudden eerie feeling that we were no longer safe inside causing goosebumps to rise on my skin. I stuck my head out into the comfortable heat of the April night, and sure enough, Janet's black Ford Escape was missing from the gravel driveway.

We called the police, and as it turned out, Sandra was never carrying triplets; she was *never even pregnant.* It was all an act so that she could get free food, free housing, and a car to steal so she and her husband could drive over the border and back into Mexico.

And then there was Aricely, one of the very few girls I actually shared a bond with. She was smart, pretty, and had a good head on her shoulders. Her only flaw, however, was that she had also fallen in love with the wrong guy. Her child's father had dumped her, but she had found love with someone else by the time her daughter was born, three months before my son arrived. She had left the home as soon as she had her baby and moved into low-income housing that she had already set up for herself in Bexar County.

Two weeks after she said her goodbyes to us girls still left behind with *nuestra señora,* and one month before Sandra had attempted to turn Janet's car into her getaway vehicle, Aricely's tear-stained face appeared on the Ten o'Clock news one night: her baby girl had been killed by her new boyfriend, who had been in the apartment to babysit while Aricely was away, providing for her daughter at a job she had just started. Months later, it would be ruled manslaughter, as the baby had cried incessantly one afternoon...and not knowing what else to do, the boyfriend (unintentionally) ended up shaking the baby out of frustration until her delicate brain collapsed against her tiny skull.

Two weeks after baby Emilia's death, Aricely appeared at *The Guadalupe Home,* her body physically there inside of the narrow foyer, but her soul departed. She politely but silently handed me her daughter's barely used car seat, matching stroller, and diaper bag since I was next in line to give birth. I never saw her again after that.

• • •

I finally left *The Guadalupe Home* in October of 1999. My time at the shelter had come to an end, as the home only provided respite for women for the duration of their pregnancies and six months thereafter to offer enough time to make new living arrangements. Janet was long gone after her car was stolen right from underneath her, and so the owners of the home hired another night shift house mother by the name of Carmen. Apparently, she had seen potential in me after we became friends, and mentioned my name to her daughter Susan, who eventually offered me a position at the architecture firm she managed in downtown San Antonio. I was to begin with the company late September of that year, and before I knew it, even weeks before I was scheduled to end my time at the home, Susan had already secured a one-bedroom apartment *and* a daycare for Caleb so that I'd be well-prepared to start my new job.

It all happened so quickly for me, like one of those things you're never ready for, but have no other choice but to put one foot in front of the other, and just...adjust.....*as quickly as possible*. The day that I was set to move out of the home, a dream I'd only been able to imagine for the past 12 months, I spent the whole morning with my face in the toilet because life was moving at the speed of light and I just knew I wasn't prepared to keep hanging on. But again, what else could I have done?

Susan was very sweet to me. If I had a doctor's appointment during work hours, she'd give me the time off and let me take her car. If she ordered lunch for us, she'd let me go pick up our goodies, and none of my time spent away from the office was counted against me. She had her hands full, though. Her 13-year-old daughter was home-schooled, but helped her mother run the show at the firm, working a normal 40-hour work week. And her four-year-old son, Matthew...? Thank God he was away at preschool for most of the day, because he was fucking nuts. Supposedly, he suffered from ADHD and took Ritalin regularly, but I never saw how the medicine helped. Every morning while on our way to Caleb's daycare and Matthew's school, Matthew would angrily kick the back of his mother's seat and spew more curse words than I could've ever come up with myself towards the back of Susan's head. I felt badly for Susan, because even though she was a sweet and accommodating mom, she didn't understand how to control the demon she gave birth to, and he was fully aware of it.

"Fuck you, bitch! I hate your fucking guts!"

It was an early Tuesday morning, and the tips of my ears actually stung at that one. I very subtly moved my hand protectively over Caleb, who sat in between me and that monster. Matthew then proceeded to throw his fists into a rage, almost successfully knocking Caleb in his chubby face.

"You stop that *right now*, Matthew Alexander!" Susan was able to snap her head back from the driver's seat and shoot a quick, angry glance at her son as the early morning traffic came to a brief pause.

"Fuck *you*!"

And all her daughter Isabel could do from the passenger seat of the aged Mercedes station wagon was stare straight ahead through the windshield, her youthful cheeks red from her mother's embarrassment, making sure we all remained calm enough on the road to get to our respective destinations safely.

I felt more sorry for Susan than I felt for myself. Her husband and the father of her kids took off two years before, leaving Susan to fend for herself against her crazy child, amongst *everything else* she had to do on her own as a single mom. Her ex still sent child support, which allowed them to live inside a fairly decent-sized apartment in one of San Antonio's ritzier neighborhoods. But she still struggled, albeit beautifully, with her children, and it was obvious her husband wanted nothing more to do with his kids outside of taking care of their financial needs.

But with the evil seed Matthew, could you blame him?

I'm wrong, I know.

Susan was doing her best, but the poor thing had no clue, and I wished that I could've been friends with her longer than I had been. Maybe I could've been a source of moral support for her. And Isabel? The girl never had a chance because she was forced to grow up way too fast, missing out on most of her mother's attention because all of it had to go to Matthew.

But I felt slightly guilty for my own thoughts every morning as I sat with Matthew in the back seat of the Mercedes. Every time he opened his hateful mouth, I would imagine myself kicking his little pre-school ass out of the car and onto the road every time his mom stopped at a red light. I was wrong, I know.

I was hired to be the receptionist at the small but lucrative firm, which employed about six white architects. They were a tight-knit community who belonged to Kingdom Hall. Susan, Isabel, and I were the only minorities and women in the office, and after a few days at my new job, I began to feel the racial tension. The owner of the company never spoke to me, unless I had to connect a call to him. He never spoke to Isabel, either; *however*, Susan got a *hello* maybe once or twice a week during the time I was employed there. The atmosphere was pretty uptight—serious and *quiet*—and I wondered if Susan was only able to keep her position there because she was damn good at what she did (and because her Mexican heritage never showed through her almost completely white skin).

I honestly don't remember what I did while I was employed in that office, but I made a decent paycheck, despite the fact I had no training outside of high school. Most of the money, though, would come in from working overtime, after the office had closed. Susan would let me stay late to help arrange and organize things in the office, the only things I was actually any good at. I sucked at answering phone calls, as I had trouble figuring out which employee to send the call to, and I never got the hang of filling out any of the records or entering the data into the computer system. Isabel was the secretary and, thankfully, sat up front with me. She had my back everytime I stumbled (which was about *all the time*). I was expected to know how to be the first point of contact for one of San Antonio's most successful architect businesses, but I felt absolutely clueless because I *was* absolutely clueless, and I knew I didn't belong.

• • •

I woke up once I felt the warm sun spread across my face and glanced at the digital clock. It was nearing 9 a.m. on a Thursday morning. But I had no more reasons to wake up early on a weekday; two months previous, I was kindly let go from my receptionist position because, according to Susan, I wasn't able to keep up with company expectations. She was right—between leaving *The Guadalupe Home*, getting my own place, putting Caleb in daycare for the first time, starting a new job, having a thirteen-year-old do better with books and finances than I ever could, and pining away for the imaginary family I still wished I had, everything became a psychotic blur for me and I was fighting a losing battle.

"I'm so sorry, Megan. I really tried to fight for you, but Richard...he wants someone with more experience."

That was the conversation Susan had with me over the phone the Sunday evening I officially got the can. "It's okay, Susan. I appreciate everything you've done for me...but I understand." And I *did* understand, and suddenly, the burden of having to get Caleb up super early in the mornings and dressed for daycare and having to fight to stay alive through Matthew's wrath was lifted from my shoulders. As I sat on the edge of my bed with the cordless phone still in my hand, I thought back to the morning when Caleb vomited twice while I was getting him and myself ready for daycare and work. I had cried through that morning because Susan was en route to my house, and I didn't know what to do: let her know that Caleb was too sick for daycare, or clean him up and just pray that he wouldn't do it again while at his school..?

I didn't know what the hell I was doing being a mom at nineteen, far away from anyone who may have cared. After I finally set the phone back onto its handset, my mother's words echoed inside my ears:

Give the baby up for adoption, tie your tubes, and have no more children.

That was said to me earlier that year, two months before I gave birth to Caleb. I cried my eyes out when I heard this over the phone, but began obediently searching for adoption agencies. I had found one, and made it as far as getting through the application to the part where Adam had to sign over his parental rights. But when I called him in Annapolis to let him know what I needed, he told me:

I'm not signing anything over until I get a test to find out if he's mine or not.

Right. The son he still had yet to meet, and Caleb was now going on ten months. That was my life on crack. Yep.

• • •

I felt a gentle tug on the sleeve of my shirt, and slightly jumped, forgetting that my sweet baby had been sleeping next to me. I turned to him and returned his toothless smile, bending over to give him his morning kisses. He moved his fat arms gleefully and giggled with me, and I wished I didn't have to pack him up and send him with his grandmother later that evening. But...losing battles. Sometimes, you just don't have what it takes to keep up the fight any longer.

Two weeks after I was fired, I took an honest look at my life, deciding to meet with an Air Force Reserves recruiter. One month later, I was sworn into the United States Military. It was now February of 2000; I was set to leave for Basic Training in 30 days.

The choice to join the military made sense. Both my parents had served; Adam was in the military; I didn't have a college education and therefore, had very limited opportunity to score that great new job that would afford the rent, the utilities, the food, the diapers, the daycare...

Since I was enlisting in the Reserves, my duty was only

part-time. I had tried my best to go active because that would've guaranteed Caleb and me more benefits, like health insurance and housing, things we desperately needed. But because I was a single mom, I was required to get Adam to sign off on the paperwork that would make him the legal guardian of Caleb, in case I were ever deployed. As of now, however, he still had yet to sign Caleb's *birth certificate*. Again, my life on crack.

I used my mother's address back in Maryland as my home address so that the military would assign me to Andrews Air Force Base in Camp Springs. My mother had agreed to allow me to stay with her until I got back on my feet, but I knew her graciousness wouldn't last long and that I would have to bust my ass to make something of myself ASAP.

The only setback: I had to sign over rights to Caleb temporarily to Veronica, who was set to arrive in San Antonio by 8 p.m. that night to pick up her grandson. I needed her to keep Caleb until I completed my basic *and* my technical training, for a total of ten weeks.

• • •

I gathered Caleb in my arms and kissed him on his forehead once more, and laid him back down to change his diaper. I thought briefly back to *The Guadalupe Home* and how even though I hated living there, I did have a support system with the other residents. I was never alone with my newborn. Never had to take on the pressure of having to figure everything out on my own when it came to being a new mom. Never had to steal quick moments from Caleb's care in order to use the bathroom or brush my teeth. And I was never at risk of succumbing to the sudden heap of turbulent postbaby hormones that threatened to do me in with their bursts of tears and sadness that left me wondering if Caleb and I were going to make it. I didn't have bills to worry over and didn't have to figure out how I was going to get food, or how I was going to get Caleb to a doctor's appointment. I was able to hold Caleb in my arms all day long, kiss him from head to little toe, sing to him, and take him out into the sunshine so he could listen to the birds sing. I was able to enjoy my baby for the first six months of his life.

Caleb was still happily babbling away by the time I was finished, and after putting his clothes back on, I carried him out to the living room and sat him on the sofa so I could prepare hot cereal for his breakfast. I drew in a slow deep breath as my eyes fell onto the huge diaper bag that sat next to him, a sad reminder of things to come. I had packed the bag two days ago in anticipation of Veronica's arrival. But as I did every day since swearing into the Air Force, I reminded myself that I was doing what was necessary to make better opportunities for my son, and at least I was doing it while his memory wasn't mature enough to remember what was happening. I remembered my father's voice from a week before and took another deep breath.

Megan, you know, you don't have to do this—

"Dad, I've signed the paperwork; I've sworn in already. They're *expecting* me." I quickly shut my mouth and pulled a deep breath in as I tried to wave off the nausea that had become a normal part of every day that followed the afternoon I signed my life away. I had felt good, *successful*, as I had raised my right hand, promising the duties that I would uphold in the U.S. Air Force Reserves. But the migraines and the constantly churning stomach–did I even *know* what the right thing was for me and Caleb?

"But I'm *telling* you, Megan...*listen* to me. If this is not something you want to do, it's not too late to get out."

I shook my head, wanting to end the conversation. Get out, and do *what*? I was at least two hours away from anyone I knew, constantly trying to keep from slitting my wrists because of the postpartum depression that had been an easy transition from my already declining mental health. Oh, and yeah—I also had a new baby to take care of by myself during one of the loneliest times of my life. Like seriously, if I didn't show up for Basic Training come March 6, then *what the fuck else was I going to do?* I didn't want to be disrespectful towards my father, but nothing he was saying was helping me. I wanted so badly to atone for my sins and make things better, and I was sorry that I put myself and my son in this mess. But it was so evident that Dad, Veronica, and even Adam, were going to make me pay for having Caleb because they all told me not to... and I did, anyway.

"I'll be alright, Dad. I'm just going through it right now because I'm so nervous about boot camp. But I'll be alright."

I pulled my eyes away from the pretty blue bag and shook my father's words out of my head, meandering around the packed boxes inside the living room to get to the small but adequate kitchen. My apartment was actually pretty beautiful, complete with my very own fireplace and a sparkling pool for the whole complex. I didn't even need to buy furniture for the place because my aunt and uncle in Austin had been moving and had generously given me most of their things. It was the perfect cozy spot for me and Caleb, and I was almost sorry to give it up. But I didn't have what it took to make it in San Antonio alone, and I wished I had been mature enough to just suck it up while I still had my job, realizing *then* that I had no choice but to do what I had to do because I was a mother, and that's what good mothers do, no matter how much they hated their circumstances. But it was *so damn hard* at nineteen to be what my son needed me to be. Poor excuse, I know. But it was the only excuse I had.

• • •

Veronica arrived promptly at 8 p.m. It was fairly warm outside, compared to what I had grown accustomed to during Februaries spent up north, so I had the baby dressed in a long blue and white fleece onesie that protected him from neck to feet, and a light windbreaker to match.

"Uh...hi, Mom. Umm, would you like to come in?"

I pulled the front door open some more so that my mother could comfortably walk over the threshold. My gesture was unnecessary, however, because she instead cocked her head to the side and spoke slowly and demurely, as always (unless she was angry). "Ah...no. Actually, the cab is right downstairs, ready to head back to the airport. So if you'll just hand me Caleb..."

What? So she was just gonna do a quick drive-by and be done with it?? I almost choked on the saliva stuck inside my throat, but remained rigor mortis stiff as was expected when facing her. It was probably for the best, though, that she got Caleb off swiftly so that we could hurry up and get this painful, and awkward, experience over and done with.

I nodded my head quickly. "Um...okay." I kept the door open while I took a few steps into the living room to retrieve Caleb's diaper bag, gently handing it over to Veronica before kissing my infant son on his cheek, then handing *him* over to his grandmother.

And with a smooth nod of her head towards me she announced: *Okay, we'll be seeing you,* and down the wooden stairs they disappeared.

For some reason, I suddenly felt like Caleb wasn't mine anymore.

The cry that erupted from deep within my insides took me by complete surprise after I closed the front door. I had no choice but to surrender to it, dropping to the carpet in agony.

5

Opportunities

My son has a permanent scar adjoining his right eye. It has lightened up significantly over the past nineteen years, but if you look closely, you can see the slightly raised and off-colored skin by the outside corner, just where Caleb's top and bottom lashes meet.

The accident happened when I went to see a career counselor at this trade school in New Carrollton, MD, which has since closed due to its never being able to obtain accreditation. I visited the school to learn about their medical assistant program since being enlisted in the military part-time was proving to be nothing but a useless pain in the ass ever since I began my journey at Andrews Air Force Base, 25 minutes away from my mother's house. Since I didn't own a car, my mother had to drive me to the base by 6 a.m. that one weekend I participated per month, *and* pick me up at 4 p.m. She'd drop me off at the Visitors' Center, which was located at the entrance to the base... about three miles away from where I had to report for duty. Andrews was *HUGE*, not like Lackland AFB in San Antonio where you could easily walk to every building. So once I got to the Visitors' Center, it was my responsibility to find someone I knew from my unit to come pick me up and take me to work.

Then I'd have to do it all over again come the end of the duty day, and wait for Veronica to come back for me, her silence during the whole car ride back to her house screaming how much of a dead weight I'd become.

And I couldn't tell you anything I did for my country during my monthly visits. All I remember is that I worked at the hospital on base in the medical records department, doing only God-knows-what while I fought my best to keep the nausea and the sensitive gag reflex in check as my anxiety made sure to show its ass when I was in the company of other Airmen. It was pointless...*I was pointless*. Leaving my little apartment in San Antonio, giving away temporary custody of my kid to his grandmother, and training with the military for a total of ten weeks did absolutely *nothing* for me. I eventually stopped going to the base, was red-lined, and subsequently placed on Inactive Reserve Duty for my remaining six years. And the *gainful employment opportunities* in the private sector that the Reserve recruiter tries to sell you for becoming a member of the Reserves—that was all bullshit. Well, at least it was for yours truly. The only opportunity I got was working for a hole-in-the-wall telemarketing gig, making about a hundred phone calls per day to beg consumers to fork over their money to charities like the Fraternal Order of Police and the local fire department.

So I packed up my two-year-old one evening and took the Metro Bus to Sanford Brown School one evening in an attempt to create *some kind* of "opportunity" for myself. You could tell that the middle-aged recruiter with the slightly rounded gut really only wanted to sell me some kind of dream of becoming a medical assistant within a year's time just to garner about $15,000 more for the dishonest school. However, I was trying my best to believe in the possibilities he was working hard to prove when, fifteen minutes into our meeting, Caleb tossed himself out of my lap in a fit of fussiness and complete boredom, and clipped his eye on the side of

Mr. Johnson's desk on his way down to the floor.

Fuck.

At first I was angry, then embarrassed, then horrified when I saw the trail of blood that quickly made its appearance. I probably should have gotten Caleb stitches that night, but we had no health insurance so I kept pressure on his eye with the sleeve of my white shirt as I told the recruiter I'd get back in touch with him (which I never did) and quickly excused myself.

And what added insult to injury (literally) was the fact that I had no idea when the next bus was coming, Caleb was still howling Bloody Mary, and it was now *raining.* I stood outside by the Metrobus stop for half an hour before deciding my transportation wasn't showing anytime soon, then hooked a ride with a complete stranger back to my mother's, hoping and praying that the man behind the wheel would not try to rape and kill me.

Me and those car rides with strangers, right?

Suffice it to say, I never returned to Sanford Brown, deciding instead to do a nursing assistant program for three months, 30 miles away in Alexandria, Virginia. My dad paid for it, and I was still able to keep Caleb in daycare while I was training. But after my mother caught wind of my father helping me (and that I was spending a little bit of money making long-distance calls to his phone (this was before long-distance was free)) she ordered me to leave her home.

"I understand that you're going to school, but after your very last day of training you are to get your belongings and find housing elsewhere."

That was Veronica. Couldn't even give me the opportunity to at least look for another fucking job before she threw my ass out again.

"And what am I going to do with Caleb?" I politely protested.

"Leave him here if you don't have another place to go."

That was what she had wanted all along. During my tenure at the small medical school, I had emailed Adam (the only form of contact he would allow me to have by this time), but he never responded. I had even gone as far as finding his *step-mother's* number to let her know I had absolutely no place to go with their grandchild. She and his father lived no more than ten minutes from my mother, actually.

"Honestly, Megan, we know that Caleb is ours, but as long as Adam continues to deny him, there's nothing we can do."

That was Shirley, Adam's step-mother since he was about three years of age. Of course I politely told her that I understood, and resumed my chase.

So on the last day of school, after I passed my written and practical exams, I took the Metrobus followed by the train back to Bowie, Maryland and got my belongings together. My sister was home, so when I put Caleb down for his usual nap, I left, like a coward, because I couldn't bear to see him cry for me as I took off without him. To this day I don't know what my mother or Avery told Caleb about my leaving so suddenly.

I stayed with a friend of mine from grade school. She had a dorm room at Trinity College in Washington, D.C. I couldn't stay there forever, but by a twist of luck (if you could call it that) I received an email from a girl named Alicia from *Adam's* email address, who claimed she had dated Adam once upon a time, had known about Caleb from the pictures I had sent him a year ago (which she'd found from hacking into his email), and wanted to extend her place to me for as long as I needed.

Her near-stalker status didn't alarm me, due to my desperation, I suppose.

"You sure you want to do this, hon?" Nicole whispered to me on the train ride back to her dorm after our meeting with Alicia.

I shrugged my shoulders, grateful that she came with me to meet this girl who had materialized out of nowhere, but knowing that I couldn't continue living in her dorm as a non-paying resident. It wasn't my smartest move, but I had no other choice. The next day, I left my friend's teeny college room and moved to Hyattsville, Maryland, which sits just down the street from Northeast, D.C. I found another job as a telemarketer (this time, selling phone plans), about 20 minutes walking distance from Alicia's apartment. My plan was to work at *Tel-ac* until I found employment as a certified nursing assistant, which would afford my own place so that I could get Caleb back from my mother.

At first, the only thing Alicia asked from me was to help out with food. Then it was, help out with half the rent. *Then* it was, help out with babysitting. She would go on and on about her history with Adam and how she was still trying to hunt him down for the bike he had promised her kid a few months back before suddenly disappearing one night. She was nuts, and I knew she was trying to make me jealous, but I remained humble and quiet during my stay at her place. And the whole time she complained about him not doing this, that, and the third for her *or* for her son, I watched her and thought:

Blah, blah-blah, blah-blaaaaaahhhhh! My life on crack, *again.*

But as always, I said nothing. I really did want to be her friend, but she would continuously vacillate between playing supportive confidante and belying the fact that she secretly hated me because she knew I'd be moving on and therefore, could no longer be her patsy. When I was finally offered a job at the hospital, I kept my plans for moving out a secret. Alicia was the kind of person you couldn't take at face value. And during the time I lived with her, I realized she couldn't maintain close relationships either because anything she said or did came with the purpose of furthering her own agenda. And after leaving her son with me to look after for a few days while she visited New York in search of another male companion to replace the mysterious Adam Hartley, I stopped pretending we could actually be friends. I had no problem helping out with rent, cooking meals, and cleaning the place. But she took it too far when she blamed me for her son catching a minor cold because I had simply forgotten to give him a hat to wear to preschool while doing *her* a favor.

I moved into my apartment that March of 2002 while she was at work. She wasn't too happy that I'd left—even tried to force me to sign over my tax return check to her so she could cash out on whatever money I supposedly owed her. Had it been a year before, I probably would've done it. But my main priority was to establish my own place and get Caleb back from my mother, and Alicia knew that from the day I met her. The hospital had just put me through a three-month class to promote me to Clinical Technician, so I was getting ready to start drawing blood and inserting IVs for my patients... and I was actually pretty damn good at what I did. So damn good that I had begun finding my confidence again, and as a result, I was starting to get so fucking sick and tired of the people who thought they had this eternal hold over me *just because* I was struggling. The shit was starting to get old when I knew I was trying my best.

That time is said and gone now. Today, I'm not sure what lesson I learned from those above experiences, if there were any lessons *to learn,* after the fact. I did the best with what I had, and yeah, Adam was able to sell me dreams just like the rounded-belly salesman at Sanford Brown had almost succeeded in doing. But I'm glad that time has passed, and once through with this memoir, I'd like to never go back to those memories that still make me shudder in guilt. But from time to time, when I glance at my oldest from his right side, I see that blemish, and I'm reminded of the thousands of ways I fucked up, and how *he* had to pay for all of them.

6

Unicorns & Fairy Dust

It was quite apparent that I had learned absolutely *nothing* inside the Southwest General Birthing Center when I had delivered Caleb without his father being present. I had called Adam shortly after Caleb joined the world, using my calling card to make the connection between San Antonio and the Coast Guard Station, Annapolis. He had sounded genuinely happy to hear from me, as I was just excited to tell him about the surprising blue eyes Caleb had come with. I remembered him chuckling quietly into the phone and jokingly asking me:

Where in the hell did he get those?

It had been a brief conversation; Adam had to get back to work minutes into the phone call. But his tender voice through the hospital phone had made me momentarily forget that I had just completed my very recent pregnancy without so much as even a Hallmark card from him during the nine months that I had carried our son. But I was nineteen-years-old, and still believed in unicorns and fairy dust. Giving birth to Adam's first child was supposed to amazingly open his heart, compel him to see that he'd been wrong for abandoning me that whole time, and make him now want to do anything he could to make up for lost time.

Excuse me as I take a moment or two to chuckle in spite of myself...

Caleb was now three, and Adam still remained at large. The last thing I heard was that he had gone AWOL from the Coast Guard, after I had filed for child support.

And now, I was pregnant, *again,* nearly six months after my stint with Alicia.

• • •

But as I stood inside the living room of my meager apartment and watched the desperation inside my new love's eyes, I was slowly beginning to see that a baby was *not* a magic potion, after all.

"I promise you...when we get married, I'll *give* you more kids. I promise. You *will* be the next Mrs. Green. I love you, but...but..."

I continued to watch Ian through burning eyes and asked quietly. "But...*what?*"

His Adam's apple moved with the effort he used to swallow, and his eyes began to flit back and forth as he searched for the answer to my question. After a moment, he positioned his eyes back onto mine, and swallowed one more time before opening his mouth. Just for a moment, I was almost sure that I saw tears in his eyes, too.

"But my parents don't even know about Caleb, Megan. So, you see, we *can't* have this baby right now."

His truth stopped my heart inside her ribcage, causing her to trip over the intricate system of veins and arteries that she beat against each millisecond of each day. I swallowed, as well, and began processing what was actually happening, jerking my hand away from Ian, not wanting him to touch me anymore. Hugging myself tightly and sniffling back the tears, I forced myself to ask:

Your parents don't know about Caleb yet? But I didn't want to know the answer.

I met Ian Green while working at Tel-ac, a piece of shit, non-sense job that served only transients, really. No employee stayed past six months, unless they were a manager... who may have then made it to *nine* months. Ian and I were both there temporarily until I finally got the position at the hospital, and he finally turned his part-time Reserve status into a full-time position at the Department of Transportation. We both ended up giving our two weeks' notices at the same time.

Ian and I just...*fit*. We had everything in common, and the things we didn't...? Those differences only served to complement the two of us and give even more depth to the chemistry we shared. We had dreams, we were driven, and we could entertain a conversation about anything and *everything*. He was so smart and so handsome, and our values and morals aligned *perfectly*. And he wrote, too—my God, could he write! It was the most refreshing thing in the world to be able to trade talents and ideas with one another—to meet each other on the same plane, in the same universe that only he and I could appreciate.

Veronica had met him one evening, actually. He had driven me back to Bowie to help assemble a small tricycle, a Christmas present I had gotten for Caleb the same year I had moved to the new apartment. I think she had been pleasantly shocked.

Ian slowly lifted himself from the fake hardwood floor, keeping his eyes on mine the whole time until he met my face. But he couldn't continue to look at me as the guilt began to cast a dark shadow across his already dark features. Looking towards his left, he responded quietly:

No. I never told my parents about Caleb.

I slanted my head to the side and parted my lips, shocked by my own ignorance, unable to respond. Ian was my first relationship since Caleb was born, and though things weren't perfect between us, I had no idea that his parents never knew about my son. As I stared open-mouthed at Ian, I quickly began to feel anger, shame, and deceit all at once. Bringing my lips back together and my head back to its center, I licked my tinted gloss and said the only thing I could think of:

Get out.

His slim face snapped back so that it was facing mine again. "Megan? *What*? No, no, *wait*...just let me explain..." He gently grabbed the sides of my arms with both of his strong hands and looked into my eyes. "No, Megan...it's not like that. You *know* how my parents are...you *know* how strict they are..."

As he rambled and begged...and begged and rambled...I thought about my three-year-old and how every time I was invited out with Ian's Haitian family, Caleb was always conveniently away with my mother for the weekends. I remembered one evening when I was at Ian's parents' house celebrating his birthday a year before, and how I had begun to tell him about my attempt earlier that day to secure child support for Caleb. But Ian had quickly raised his index finger to his mouth, and with a subtle shake of his head, directed me to keep quiet. But I never put two and two together until that moment.

I wasn't good enough for the only man who had ever validated all of the good parts about me, while keeping his focus off the bad. Who did I hate for this? Adam? Myself? My mother? Ian...?

"...but ultimately, the decision is up to you..."

Yeah right. I stepped away, no longer knowing the man who was standing in front of me. His arms dropped by his sides. Turning away, I fixed my eyes on the living room's small window and gazed outside to Ian's black, late model Acura sedan, parked parallel to the apartment, the prettiest thing in the tired complex.

"Get out."

I felt him hesitate behind me for a minute before he blew out a quiet breath and muttered *fine* softly and frustratingly. After some shuffling behind me, I was disappointed when I heard the jingling of his set of keys before he finally opened the door and let it close behind him. I didn't want him to leave; I honestly wanted him to stay and try to empathize with my side of the story. To see my tears and feel my pain and understand that what he was asking me to do was wrong, and that he would stay until we arrived at a decision we *both* could live with. But I had to be strong in front of him and prove that I wasn't going to let him knock me off my square, that I was better than how he was treating me, and that I was *completely fucked up with him* for begging me to kill his child.

I tried my hardest after having Caleb. But that would never matter to anyone.

When I watched him finally pull off from the side of the curb and down the street, back to his cozy home and to a reality that didn't belong to me, I let the blinds close and trudged to the only bedroom in the house. Collapsing in non-stop cries upon the bed Caleb and I shared, memories of my time with Ian over the past year and a half flooded my mind as I sought to understand why in the world he had to wait to marry me when he could just do it right then, if he really wanted to.

Because his parents don't know that you're already a mama, that's why.

I squeezed my eyes shut, trying to block the voice inside my head. Ian and I were both twenty-two, we both had decent jobs at the time, and he had his family home while I had my apartment (no matter how small it was). I wasn't doing so badly for having a small child. Ian and I could get married, join our two incomes, and live happily ever after with Caleb and the new baby (even though

Caleb was completely nonexistent to Ian's parents)...

There I go again, *unicorns and fairy dust.*

As the sun began to cast an orange glow across the bedroom, indicating the end of day, my heart sank into the pit of my belly as I tried to figure out why nobody wanted me or Caleb.

• • •

Two weeks later, Ian and I were in the waiting room of *The Family Reproductive Center,* which was code for: abortion clinic. The procedure was $290, and Ian had already paid for it. As I waited with the other young women who had obviously made the same mistake I had, my sandled foot tapped uncontrollably alongside the erratic beating of my heart.

I took slow deep breaths as the doctor pried my cervix open with a speculum, while silently convincing myself that I was doing the right thing because it made no sense to keep a pregnancy the father didn't want, not again. When I heard the motor of the large vacuum system switch on, I bit down on my lower lip, making sure to hold my breath every time I felt the suctioning of my insides. I felt sick to my stomach with each forceful push of air into my uterus, but after five minutes, it was over.

Ian was waiting inside the adjoining recovery room, and when I saw him, I immediately fell into his chest. He held onto me tightly and let me cry out my pain and regret against his dark blue t-shirt. I hated him for not having to experience the torture that only *I* had to feel, but I hated *myself* even more for getting pregnant, once again, and having no other choice but to kill an innocent part of me.

• • •

I should've seen the end of our relationship coming. In the month following the abortion I grew despondent as the world outside my apartment door seemed to recede further and further from my grasp, leaving me and Caleb inside of a darkness that was ours alone. I saw Ian less and less, and on the days that we did spend time together, he was impatient, as if being with me was now an obligation of his. Like the morning we attended Sunday Mass, a tradition we kept for most of our relationship. As usual, after the service, we visited the crypt of the basilica, wandering around together as a family (the weekends that I had Caleb), stopping at each chapel to admire the statues and the small, but ornately decorated prayer rooms. But as I walked on that particular Sunday, I couldn't help but notice that Ian kept mostly to himself...and checked his watch every five minutes.

When we finally made it back to my home, my heart dropped when he told me that he'd see me later. Another custom we kept on Sundays was to have lunch together at the apartment.

"You're *leaving*?"

His dark eyes took on that distressed look again as he lowered his head into my space to make sure I understood what he was about to say. "Megan, I gotta go. I can't always be with you all the time—"

"—but you always stay after Mass..."

He paused before rolling his eyes to the ceiling and retreating his head, and my heart began beating faster inside my belly as the fear of his leaving me forever was quickly manifesting. He put his hands on his waist and blew out an impatient breath. "Megan...I can't be there for you all the time. I just can't do—"

"Can I have a cookie, Mommy?"

I looked down at my son, who was tugging gently on my dress, a pale yellow piece I had carefully chosen hours before to secretly keep Ian by my side, knowing deep down that our relationship had already been doomed the very second I stepped foot inside *The Family Reproductive Center.* "Sure, Caleb, go ahead in the kitchen and get a cookie." When I made sure Caleb couldn't hear me, I looked back at Ian. "You can't do *what,* Ian?"

"I can't *do this* anymore, Megan!" He let his hands go and stepped away from me as if he were suddenly made aware of some kind of contagious disease I had. He started pacing the floor, and I couldn't help but wonder if he had rehearsed this scene before picking Caleb and me up for Mass.

He stopped in the middle of the living room and turned towards me. "I can't do this anymore. I can't always be there for you like you require me to be. I can't be your savior...and I'm *definitely* not ready for a family. At least, not right now. I mean, *my God*—I'm only *twenty-two-years-old!*"

"What?" My voice came out in a squeak, and I started to shake. I had to wrap my arms around my middle in order to keep my fragile psyche together. The tears started, but I had to stop them because I wasn't going to show my son—or Ian—how weak I actually was. I swallowed them down and pointed angrily at Ian, keeping my voice low. "You told me that if I did this for you, you were going to marry me...you were going to give me more children. Why did you *lie* to me?"

He rolled his eyes upwards again and breathed out that annoying puff of air, failing to give an answer, because there *was* no answer. This had all been a part of his plan: making sure I got rid of the pregnancy because he knew he didn't see a forever with us in his future. It was all part of his plan.

"I can't do this...you want too much from me. I mean, I'm not ready to be a father to Caleb, and yet, you want *everything* from me! Megan, I'm not even *your husband.*"

Wow. I turned to the small living room window before the tears left my eyes and reached my burning cheeks, choosing to focus on Ian's pretty black Acura. The abortion was just the very beginning of an inevitable ending that I was too stupid to see coming. I swallowed, keeping my composure, and whispered:

Get out then since Caleb and I are such a problem.

I heard him take a step towards me. "So that's what you really want?"

He didn't even have the integrity to just tell the truth. The abortion was already done and over with; he was now a free man. I kept quiet and continued to focus on his car.

I heard him take another frustrated sigh (or was that a sigh of relief?) before he quietly opened and shut the apartment door behind him. He didn't even say goodbye to Caleb.

I continued to watch through the window, silently praying that I wouldn't actually see him leave the front of the building... that he would think twice and come back to the apartment. I never wanted him to go because I *needed* him to fill that crater that was left when Adam and the rest of my family and friends ditched me when I got pregnant with my son. I didn't know what else I was going to do because being alone meant that I was a nobody. It meant that no matter how hard I worked to provide a better life for Caleb, I was never going to be good enough to meet anyone's standards because the 'single mom' mark was branded to me for life. But I told Ian to leave because that's what any woman with even a *quarter* of self-esteem would do. And I had to make him believe that *I* believed I deserved better, forcing him to finally realize that he really didn't want to leave my life and that this was only a grave misunderstanding between two hurt people.

I watched as Ian finally emerged from the entrance to the apartment and into my line of sight. He walked with his head hung low and his hands stuffed inside his dress pants, never looking back.

"Him"

He was my drug.

I wasn't addicted to
Cocaine,
Heroin,
or
Methamphetamine...

I wasn't even addicted to
Alcohol,
Pills,
Or
Sex...

I was addicted to *him*.

Felt like a wreck
When he was gone,
Knew he was
Horrible–
But could never get enough.

He was my Super-Drug.
Only a person,
But still the medication
That made me feel like a
Superwoman.

I laughed when I was with him,
Cried when he was with *them*.
Tried one day
To quit him,
Cold turkey–

But just as an addict
Tries to up and quit,
The chills and the nausea
Proved stronger than
My need to let go.

So I continued to drink
My elixir–
To inhale its seductive scent,
To wallow in its
Deceptive Charm–

Until one day...

I got up and made the decision
To finally quit:
To quit this substance forever,
And to finally get help
To rid this thing from my life.

I was dressed–
I was ready to go and
Seek expert guidance,
Until I opened my door,
And there he stood...

And I let him in.

7

Meal Ticket

I loved Mateo because my mother hated me...because Ian broke up with me after our abortion...and because Adam had nothing to do with me since I first told him I was pregnant. Mateo made it clear to me from the beginning that he wasn't looking for a relationship, but I needed him for my emotional wreckage, so it was more than easy to attach myself to him and hold onto him as hard as I could (whenever he was available, that is).

I had become a human parasite, and never realized it.

I met Mateo James at his job at VEIP (Vehicle Emissions Inspection Program) when I took my car there to get it checked for harmful emissions, a Maryland state requirement every two years. It was March of 2003, and I was starting life nearly all over again after having to give up the apartment Ian had leased for me for almost a year. I had terminated our pregnancy due to his request, but didn't realize at the time that ending the life inside of me was just the beginning of the end for me and him.

He had begged me to get the abortion because at the end of the day, I wouldn't have been good enough since I already had Caleb. Dating a nearly-unhinged woman who already had a child, and then having to get her an apartment was already enough. Add a new baby to the mix...? In my fairy tale, make-believe world, it would have made sense. However, there was no way on God's green earth that Ian could possibly tell Mom and Dad that he was expecting, and, oh, by the way... *Megan already has a kid.*

I promise you...when we get married, I'll give you more kids. I promise. You will be the next Mrs. Green. I love you, but...but...

• • •

Ian had leased the apartment Caleb and I were living in back in Hyattsville. When I was living with Alicia, I didn't have enough credit (or money), and the original plan was for us to get a place together. However, after the leasing agent told us that the lease could be in *his* name only, the plan changed and Ian decided *not* to move in with me. But he did sign the lease, kept a key, and paid half the rent for the six months I was there.

I'm sorry I wasn't good enough to keep him with me forever...

My credit status had nothing to do with his suddenly not wanting us to share a home. He just realized that had he moved in with Megan-*the-temptress*, his parents would have finally learned that I had Caleb.

Jesus, I was never going to be good enough for anyone, was I?

After I had the abortion, we parted ways. Three months later, he used his active military orders to break the lease and moved to Jersey. Having nowhere else to go, I had to ask my mother if Caleb and I could room with her until further notice. She *very* reluctantly agreed. I knew she never wanted to see me back at her place again, but I was just so grateful to have a roof over our heads that her dreadful opinion of me didn't even matter.

Well, *maybe* it didn't even matter *that* much...

. . .

"Megan." My mother lifted her head and looked at me with her sharp eyes and spoke quietly but dramatically. She should've been an actress. "What am I supposed to do with only $250? There's the mortgage, the groceries, the electricity..."

*Yeah, and Caleb's daycare, my car note, my insurance, the gas for my damn car, and the money that I need to put away so that I can relieve you of your burden...*I pulled in a slow, subtle breath, careful not to let my mother see my frustration through the rise of my chest, moving my eyes away from her to glance at Caleb, who was busy with his toy fire truck. It was another Friday payday for me, and as always, the $250 I gave her faithfully was never enough. As sure as I knew Adam was never going to lay eyes on Caleb again, I also knew that I couldn't do anything right by Veronica. And every day that I was in her house, I felt more and more like the unwelcome house guest who'd more than overstayed her welcome after the very first night spent in the guest bedroom. Every other Friday evening, I'd respectfully give her the withdrawal I made from my account and watch her count the cash slowly between her long and slender fingers as I held my breath in anticipation of her disapproval.

I let out my breath so that I could answer her question, still careful to make sure she didn't see my frustration and told her the same thing I'd been telling her for the past four months. "Sorry, Mom, but that's all I can afford right now." God, I hated how my voice trembled in front of her.

Veronica kept her eyes on me, and it was all I could do not to completely come apart from the pressure to be anyone other than the person that my mother despised. Her powerful gaze cut me, and I wished, as I always had since I was a little girl, that I could become worthy of her approval. But it was clear that she was going to hold my baby-making mistakes against me for as long as I breathed air.

And in the meantime, Caleb's father Adam got to skate away scot-free while I struggled alone for something he and I *both* were a part of.

• • •

Mateo James was a cool and confident—almost arrogant...no, *definitely* arrogant—type of guy. The kind that you'd want as a good friend because he was charming, carried his charisma with him everywhere he went, and he could make a joke out of anything. But he wasn't right for me. He was a hard worker at VEIP, but after his shifts ended, he clipped a glock pistol to his hip and sold benzos and other mind-altering drugs well into the unsafe hours of the night. I had no clue that I was getting in way over my head until I started meeting Mateo every Wednesday on my weekday off from the hospital. I'd drop Caleb off at his daycare, eagerly drive the 20 miles to Mateo's apartment, we'd make love, grab breakfast, then I'd drop him off at his job. When he got off in the evenings, I'd be waiting for him inside VEIP's parking lot, with Caleb in tow, and let him drive my Nissan Sentra into D.C. so he could make his stops on the Southeast side. Caleb would be secured in his carseat, and I'd be in the passenger seat of my own car, holding back my motion sickness, while Mateo would drive a few miles, stop at a corner, get out, exchange his product, drive a little more ways, stop at another corner, get out, exchange the drugs, get back in, drive some more...and, well...you get the picture.

Mostly, he sold marijuana (this was years before it was finally legalized in the District) and Xanax and Valium. He was the real-deal, real-life, bad boy, and though he would never *ever*, in a million and one years be my type, he was able to take my mind away from the failure I'd become during the four years of my son's existence.

I didn't like being out in the streets with Mateo. Felt like a shitty-ass mother for subjecting my son to his lifestyle of crime, and in the very deep parts of my mind, I knew I couldn't actually be in love with a man like him. Mateo was almost like Veronica. I was out to please both of them, though I never succeeded. I wanted my mother to see that I was an actual person, more than the mistakes I had made in my past. And I wanted Mateo to love me for me and to *want* a relationship with me. But almost anything was better than being at home with Veronica and her endless looks of disapproval and distaste. Whereas Veronica made me feel like I should be stoned for having a kid outside of marriage, Mateo never made any deal out of the fact that I was a mother at twenty-two, and at the time, that meant more to me than subjecting my preschooler to Mateo's petty misdemeanors. I *liked* that he needed me. *Liked* the fact that I finally had *something* to offer to somebody else, and that I didn't have to feel like I was worthless because of the choices I'd made in my past that didn't suit everyone else.

• • •

"So why do you do this at night, when you already make a decent paycheck with your job at VEIP?" I had asked him one night after dropping him off at home.

He ducked down and placed his head by the open window of my driver's side, and the scent of his cologne mixed with the sweat earned from hustling earlier made my heart float. He slowly shrugged his shoulders while piercing me with his dark eyes and responded:

I told you, Megan, you'd never understand.

And with that, he tenderly kissed the side of my cheek and

told me, "Thanks again for the ride." He nodded towards Caleb, who had fallen asleep in the back of the car. "Now get Shorty home 'cause it's late."

• • •

One day I informed my mother of my desire to cut back my hours and my days at work and begin school at the local community college. As soon as the schedule became available for me at the hospital, I planned to put in my request to work 12-hour shifts Friday, Saturday, and Sunday so that I could register for one or two classes to start off with. Much to my surprise, however, Veronica lifted her head from the book she was reading and calmly told me:

Megan. You gave up your right to go to school the day you decided to become a mother.

What a fucking hypocrite. *She* had finished her bachelor's way after I was born, but I guess it was acceptable for her back then since she had been *married*.

I had believed she would be delighted to see me doing something other than taking orders from nurses and serving as somebody's "assistant" at the hospital. Veronica had actually been the one who inspired my love of academia through her never-ending pursuit of learning. And no matter what I've revealed through these pages, this will be something I will always admire. However, living with my mother forced me to realize that it was never her desire to see me surpass the stereotypes she was intent on branding me with. I loved my mother and I wanted to be as successful as she was, but I also hated her for making it so easy for me to hate what I saw in the mirror each and every day

• • •

"What do you wanna eat?"

I looked towards Mateo, whose 5'7" height surpassed mine by almost four inches, and studied his profile while he gazed at Burger King's breakfast menu. He was about 150 pounds, slender frame, midnight black skin, a squarish and perfectly chiseled head, clean, low haircut, and a trimmed mustache that brought out the thickness and kissable-ness of his lips. His dark handsomeness effortlessly stood out in a room full of people. As he kept both hands deep inside the pockets of his dark denim jeans, he pretended not to notice the attention he was getting from me *and* the girl at the cash register, who patiently and happily waited for him to give her our order, as the blush spread atop her light cheeks. I turned back to the menu, deciding on just a coffee and some tater tots.

"That's all you want?"

I turned back to Mateo, as he turned to face me, and I almost died when his eyes, made overcast by the shadow from his fitted baseball cap, met mine. "Yeah, that's all I want."

"You sure?" He continued to watch me, and I couldn't tell... but I thought that I saw a smile begin to separate the corners of his mouth, something he did very rarely with me as he tried to keep whatever feelings he had for me (if any) to himself.

I turned back towards the menu of breakfast croissants and flavored coffees and nodded towards the cashier. "Yep, I'm sure."

"Alllriiighhhttt." From my left peripheral, Mateo placed his attention back towards the cashier. "Give me your number two, Miss, a large orange juice with that, and a large French Vanilla coffee and some of your tater tots for Shorty over here."

My face warmed from the flutters of butterflies in the pit of my stomach and the undeniable infatuation in my heart when I heard the *Shorty* part. I turned back towards Mateo, who was now casually plucking out ones and fives from a thick bundle of cash he had pulled from his back jeans pocket. The time was nearing 9:30 in the morning and Mateo and I were on our weekly Wednesday morning dates. After dropping Caleb off at his daycare, I drove the 15 miles to Mateo's apartment to pick him up for breakfast. Last week was IHOP; this week was Burger King. It was our routine, and I relished every moment of it.

"Here you go, Miss. That's thirteen, eighty nine, exactly." Mateo politely laid his payment inside of the cashier's eager palm before taking the receipt she in turn handed him. When he placed his hand lightly on the middle of my back to guide me away from the registers so we could wait for our food, a surge of electricity traveled the length of my spine.

$$\bullet \bullet \bullet$$

Veronica was waiting for me when I finally got home that afternoon after dropping Mateo off at work.

"I just wanted you to know that for Caleb's birthday, I'm taking him to the Baltimore Aquarium."

I squinted in confusion at my mother. No, *How 'bout we take Caleb out for his birthday,* or, *Do you have plans for Caleb's birthday (since he is YOUR son)?* Or, *Is it okay with you that I take Caleb to the aquarium for his birthday?* But I knew better than to say anything other than *Okay* to Veronica because I was living in *her* house and if she wanted to strip me of my parental rights, that was her prerogative.

The following day was Caleb's fourth birthday, and true to Veronica's word, she left with her grandson early that morning to head out to Baltimore, leaving me just enough time to make him breakfast and dress him appropriately. I did have plans for my son, but a trip to his favorite toy store and lunch afterwards was apparently nothing compared to Veronica's birthday itinerary. However,

I assured myself that as long as Caleb was happy, it didn't matter who took him out for his birthday. And he seemed pretty excited after I finished dressing him for the day. When he was finally out the door, Veronica barely made eye contact with me as she mentioned something about returning later that evening. I imagined her getting a kick out of being able to show me who was actually in charge.

Once the door closed behind my mother and son, there was nothing but me and the silence left behind as I stood, dumbstruck, in the middle of my mother's pristine living room. Suddenly, I felt like I had no place inside Veronica's house without Caleb being there, so I made my way to the guest bedroom and rested on the corner of the bed for a moment. My mind drifted to Caleb's paternal grandmother, Ava, and how she had never met her first grandchild because she was against me continuing with the pregnancy in the first place. I had only met Adam's mom one time before I conceived Caleb, and she had seemed nice enough, but people change when there's suddenly a baby on the way.

"My baby is *not* gonna take care of *your* baby!" she had screamed at me through the phone before offering to pay for an abortion. *Jesus Christ*, her 'baby' was twenty-two-years-old when I got pregnant. But she had been absolutely right at the time—the only thing Adam ever did in four years was leave a week's worth of daycare tuition at the front door of Veronica's house almost two years ago.

Damn.

With a sigh I turned away from my thoughts and with nothing else to do that early in the morning, and not wanting to continue feeling like an intruder inside my mother's house, I showered, threw some clothes on, and got into my car. I didn't know exactly where I was going, but the April weather was a breath of fresh

79

air, and I enjoyed sitting behind the wheel. It was just something about being inside my car, alone with the road and my thoughts, that made me feel as free as an eagle. Five miles down the street, I decided to stop at Starbucks for a vanilla latte, and an hour after that, I was at the Toys R Us in New Carrollton, shopping for Caleb's birthday present. Turned out, I wasn't too far from Mateo's job, and it *was* nearing the time he usually got off, so when I was finished picking out Caleb's gift, I decided to take my chances and head on over to see if Mateo wanted a ride back to his place. I knew it'd be a chance I was taking because technically, I wasn't Mateo's girlfriend. *Technically*, he could've had plans after work that didn't include me, because Wednesdays were our hang-out days, and today was *Thursday*. And *technically*, none of that even mattered to me because life at Veronica's *sucked ass*, and I didn't want to be anywhere around it if I didn't need to be.

He was surprised but happy to see me. And, for once, we didn't head out to the southeast block to hustle his product. I wasn't an expert in the art of selling street meds, but it didn't make much sense to me for Mateo to keep putting his life and freedom at risk every night to make a little bit of pocket change, without really having anything to show for it. But who was I to judge? I was a twenty-three-year-old, unwed, single mother to a kid whose only immediate family consisted of a mother-and-grandmother duo who couldn't learn to put their differences aside for the well-being of said kid. Oh, and I was also still a year away from my official mental health diagnosis, and had yet to learn the art of self-medicating.

We actually had a real date, at night, at an outdoor restaurant, where I could finally let my hair down and pretend that I was *somebody* for a moment.

Dinner was finished by nine, and when I dropped Mateo back at his place in Temple Hills, he handed me a $20 bill through the opened driver's side window:

"Here, give this to Shorty for his birthday."

As usual, he kissed me on the side of my cheek and thanked me for taking him home.

• • •

"You know, you could've at least been here when we got home."

That was Veronica's greeting to me when I made it back to Bowie at 9:40 that night. Caleb was already upstairs for the evening, and I still had yet to give him his gift, which was tucked away inside my bag.

I let out an audible breath and leaned over to take off my tennis shoes. "Mom, I had no idea when you guys were getting home."

"You could've called, you know—"

Yeah, and so could you. I reached into my bag and pulled out my cell, opening it to make sure I didn't miss any calls from Veronica while I had been out, already knowing that I didn't. I closed my phone and gently shook my head. "Okay, Mom. Sorry." I moved to the fridge and grabbed a bottled water, feeling my mother's eyes burn holes into the side of my face as she stood close to the kitchen entrance's frame, arms folded over her chest as she, no doubt, scrambled furiously about what to come up with next.

"And where *were* you all day?"

I placed the water on the marble countertop and slowly began to turn its lid. My profile still facing my mother, I carefully looked up to the kitchen's ceiling—making sure it didn't appear as if I were rolling my eyes at the woman—and wondered why God didn't just take me then. I concentrated back on my water, finally getting the top off. "I went out to dinner and hit traffic on my way here–"

"— and you couldn't find anything appropriate to wear other than *that*?"

Jesus of Nazareth! I looked down at my outfit—a form-fitting, white rayon, v-neck tee over a pair of pink Bermuda shorts. "Mom, it was *hot* outside earlier—what's wrong with what I'm wearing?"

Nothing was wrong with it, so instead of answering my question, she gave a *Hmph* and a dramatic shake of her head before saying, "You know, you could've at least had a cake ready for your son's birthday. Or a cookie, or at *least* a cupcake. *Anything* since I had him with me all day today."

Sonofabitch! I suddenly slammed down the plastic bottle of water onto the countertop, not caring about the liquid that splashed over the top of the bottle's rim. I faced my mother, and in the blink of an eye, she looked surprised at my reaction, but she quickly straightened herself up to regain her control.

I spoke slowly. "Mom. I have his present inside my bag. There was no one here, so I left for a few."

I watched her as she blinked her eyes once or twice and cleared her throat. "Megan. That's still no excuse." Her frosty eyes began to shrink into slits as she peered harder at me. "You know, I'm beginning to think that you use that poor, innocent boy as your meal ticket. Why don't you just do him a favor and leave him with me?"

Meal ticket?

"And leave my son, just like that, Mom?"

"Yes, 'just like that' because we both know that you're not fit enough to be a mother to him."

Fuck you, fuck you, FUCK YOU! The anger in my blood began to flood my body, and all I wanted to do was lunge the opened bottle of water at Veronica to see if its contents would wash out the smug expression she wore on her perfectly painted face. But in twenty-three years, I'd never even yelled at my mother, let alone thrown water bottles at her. So before I totally lost it with her, I swallowed my pride and my pain and respectfully told her:

"I'll get out of your hair then." Leaving the water on the countertop, I gathered my shoes and exited the kitchen, my fractured heart pumping hard underneath my rib cage, as I kept my head down so that she wouldn't get the pleasure of seeing my wet eyes. When I reached the bottom of the staircase leading up to the guest bedroom, I heard her call out behind me:

"And if you even *think* of taking Caleb with you, I'll report you to the police for being an unfit mother!"

Go to hell!

8

That Thing

When you unexpectedly run low on available options, you find yourself making decisions you otherwise would have never made. Or maybe, that just applied to me alone.

I was forced to move in with Mateo because my mother didn't want me in her home anymore. And conveniently, Mateo had just lost his job at the Maryland Vehicle Emissions station for being a no-call, no show after being thrown in lock-up for two days after his part-time job as a (very) small-time drug dealer finally caught up with him.

Maybe I should've left Caleb with my mother, but I couldn't imagine walking away from him again. Veronica wanted to back me into a corner where I had no other choice *but* to leave my son with her; however, she underestimated the love I had for Caleb. She tried so hard to make me out to be this mother who only had a kid in order to use him...in order to have excuses to be lazy so the government could take care of her...somebody who didn't give a *shit* about her offspring. But that had never been me, and she should have known better because she didn't raise me to be like that. As hard as it had been to carry Caleb and give birth to him on my own, why *the fuck* would I end up throwing him by the wayside, like he never ever mattered, just to get on this welfare that I had never taken advantage of *in the first place*? I was supposed to go to college before I had completely caved in to the control my mother had over me. I was supposed to go to art school and become this *amazing* artist in New York. Ambition had always come easily to me, and yet, Veronica worked hard to turn me into some kind of stupid, but cunning, woman who could only be as ambitious as her vagina allowed, like I didn't have anything else going for me. So yeah, lie down and get pregnant, and then use the *baby* as an excuse to continue being a lazy fuck-up, when I hadn't been one in the first fucking place!

And the ironic thing is, I didn't even *like* sex back then.

So, you see, that thing...that thing that people try to brand you with for the choices you've made that they don't agree with...? That thing that has people *forcing* these labels onto your character, that compels them to *make* you into what they expect you to be...? That fucking *thing*!

Because of *that thing,* I never had a chance with Veronica, no matter how much money I gave her, no matter what kind of job I had, no matter if *I took home the Mother of the Year Award every fucking year.* I never had a chance.

After Veronica had demanded, for the fiftieth time since I'd moved back in with her almost a year prior, that I leave Caleb with her and go on with my life, I angrily packed an overnight bag for me and Caleb and called Mateo to see if I could crash at his place. But he wasn't home, and he didn't have a cell phone, so all I could do was hide out in the guest bedroom for the weekend and stay out of my mother's way. I couldn't even seek the solace that my job often provided because I didn't have to be at work for the weekend. By the time I had finally received word that Mateo was still alive and well, it was on a Thursday afternoon, via a phone call from his lawyer.

"Hello?"

"Hello, may I please speak to Megan Harris?"

Not recognizing the voice, I answered cautiously. "Yes, this is she..."

"Well, I'm Mr. Stanley, and I'm here with Mr. James at the courthouse, and he's going to need a ride home."

My eyebrows met in the middle. "Mateo? A ride home? For what?"

"Well, Ms. Harris, he was arrested two days ago for marijuana possession and assault and battery–"

"— *assault and battery*...?"

On the other end of the line, I waited for Mr.Stanley to clear his throat. "Well, um...he assaulted a police officer, ma'am."

I rubbed my right temple and sighed deeply into my phone. Assault and possession? So that's why I hadn't heard from Mateo in about a week. I looked over at Caleb who was trying to pull on a pair of shoes I had asked the salesman for before my phone rang. I knew I'd be wrong for cutting my afternoon date with Caleb short, but the grip Mateo had on anything inside of me that made any kind of sense was almost supernatural. And even though I knew I shouldn't get involved with his shit, I was stupidly devoted to the fact that he needed me. I asked Mr. Stanley for the address, paid for the gray pair of sneakers for Caleb, and got ready to head into the District.

I tried to ignore the smart part of me—the quieter side that lives deep within everyone, who's there to make sure they don't fuck up—but she nagged me all the way down to the courthouse. I knew I should've told Mr. Stanley that I was busy...that my car was in the shop...that I needed to pick up my son from daycare... *anything* other than *I'd be right there.* I thought about turning my car back around a few times, but you see, being with Mateo took my mind away from something I could never measure up to, in the eyes of my mother. Being around Mateo validated my self-worth.

I stalled the car next to the sidewalk of 500 Indiana Avenue, NW for ten minutes before Mateo appeared, his squarish head downcast and his charismatic character temporarily absent. He was still in his navy blue coveralls that he wore for work, meaning he had gone out to hustle straight after leaving his job, as was his usual, before he was arrested. I sighed as he slowly pulled open my car's passenger door, the smell of filthy body odor mixed with defeat as he quietly sat down in the car.

"Sorry I smell so bad, but they don't let you take showers in jail, let alone let you even piss without nobody looking."

I grimaced and nodded my head. "It's okay."

We arrived at Mateo's apartment twenty minutes later, shortly after crossing the D.C./Maryland border. I proceeded to pull up to the front of his building to let him out, but he turned to me and asked if I wanted to come in. I was surprised; Mateo liked his privacy, or at least, he liked his privacy away from *me*. I had sex with Mateo, had Wednesday morning breakfast dates with Mateo, and let him use my car after work so he could make extra money on the street corner. Well...*once* we did have that impromptu dinner one night...and for my 23rd birthday, he *did* treat me to a *real* date, complete with dinner and a movie afterwards. But Mateo always made sure I understood that he didn't want a girlfriend, and I accepted this because I was between a rock and a hard place with my mother while stealing moments of Mateo's time. And in between those two places, there was no other place to go.

Of course I took Mateo up on his offer, but I felt guilty knowing that I was a mother and therefore, I shouldn't have had Caleb there with me. Caleb was just four—he had a certain bath time, a certain dinner time, and a certain prayer time. We couldn't do all those things at Mateo's place.

Caleb had fallen asleep in the back of the car, so Mateo reached to unbuckle him from his carseat and gathered him carefully in his arms before carrying him up the two flights of steps to his apartment door. Once inside, he quietly and swiftly headed to his bedroom towards the back and laid Caleb down to sleep.

He ran a bubble bath for me and instructed me to get in, that I looked as if I needed to relax. I was surprised by his sudden gentleness, but I didn't question it because I was content with whatever Mateo offered me at that moment, because I felt *lucky*.

I called my mother to let her know where Caleb and I would be for the night. She didn't answer—big surprise—so I left her a voicemail. I knew she wouldn't care (at least, not about *my* whereabouts), but since I lived in her house, I wanted to be respectful.

• • •

My nerves began to settle some once my body made contact with the hot water, and as I watched Mateo calmy kick off his dingy coveralls and pull his white t-shirt over his head, I became mesmerized. When he got into the tub behind me and gently guided me back towards his chest, I wanted the evening to last forever. I closed my eyes as he began to speak into my ear.

"Thank you for gettin' me today. I didn't know who else to call..."

"It's okay."

"Megan...?"

"Yep?"

I heard him take a breath from behind me. "I got fired today."

My eyelids flew open and I quickly turned my back towards Mateo, splashing some of the water over the top of the tub. "You

My sleepy eyes expanded and I instantly turned to face Mateo, splashing some of the water over the top of the tub. *"You got fired?"*

He turned me back around so that I was facing the front of the tub again. I heard him sigh once more and then I heard the click of a bottle before feeling the watery silkiness of body wash across my back, quietly wondering why the soap smelled like raspberry souffle, but refusing to linger on anything that may sabotage the moment. "I got fired for being a no-call, no-show. I wasn't able to call them from jail and let them know that I was locked up."

"So what are you going to do now?"

He sighed again. "I don't fucking know, Megan." He kept his voice low as he continued to wash me. He softly bit my earlobe. "I missed you."

I didn't respond. Just rested against Mateo's slender but strong chest and enjoyed the quiet splashing of the bath water and the security that I wanted desperately to believe Mateo would provide for me.

"I am so in love with you, Megan..."

I closed my eyes again and kept my mouth shut, knowing that Mateo only said it because I came to pick him up from the court building. Seconds later, I heard myself asking, "Why did you get arrested?"

For a moment, he said nothing, and all that could be heard was the steady *thump-thump* of his heart beating against my back.

He took another breath and answered: "I had some weed on me, and when I went to run, the arresting officer grabbed me and tackled me to the ground. But, Megan, I *swear* I didn't hit him." He sat up and showed me his right arm. "You see all these scratches and cuts right here? This shit is all from the officer who caught me while I was tryna run."

I examined the several cuts that wrapped around his smooth,

midnight forearms. "And what about the weed?"

Mateo smirked. "No, they were right about the weed. I *did* have that on me. I'm just mad they took it from me. I was supposed to smoke that shit that night." He gave a hearty laugh that echoed inside the bathroom.

I smiled. His amusement in spite of his earlier ordeal was contagious and I wanted to laugh with him, even though I knew this whole situation was just *wrong*, and that I should probably haul my ass out of the tub, throw my clothes back on, collect my son, and leave. But instead, I shook all reason from my head and jokingly pursed my lips together, silently admonishing him. I didn't care about the weed, though, or about his pending charges; I was just glad to be in his presence. I turned back towards the front of the tub and relaxed myself against Mateo's comforting strength. I closed my eyes again as he began to draw his fingers through my hair in an effort to detangle it.

"Why don't you move in here with me?"

I choked on my saliva. He said the words so softly that I wondered if I was hearing things. I moved up in the tub and faced his dark eyes once again. "What did you say?"

"Why don't you move in here with me?"

"Me and Caleb?"

He sighed, clearly annoyed by my asking questions that should've had obvious answers. "Yes, Megan. You and Caleb."

I lied back down against his chest and chose my words carefully, not wanting to ruin our night. "I thought you were completely against the whole 'girlfriend thing'...?" I waited for an answer, but got nothing in return. When I turned to take a look at him, his head was against the tub's wall and his eyes were closed.

• • •

When Caleb and I returned to my mother's that Saturday morning, my key didn't work.

"What the hell...?"

"Mommy, *don't* say that."

I looked down at my son's innocent face and gave him a nervous chuckle. "I'm sorry, darling. You're right." I turned my attention back to the door and tried the house key for another two minutes. Nothing.

Reluctantly, I softly knocked on my mother's door, hating ever having to go back to her house. I hated every damn thing about that stupid house. Hated the dirty looks my mother gave me whenever I was around...hated the way she thought I was a waste of space and that I would never amount to anything because I had Caleb at a young age. I even hated the *scent* of the house. *Shit*! I was trying my fucking best by working and trying to start college—I was even giving her nearly half my paycheck every two weeks. *What more did she want from me?*

My heart jumped when I heard the slow turn of the door knob from the inside. I clenched Caleb's hand a little tighter and forced myself to look into the coolness of my mother's light brown eyes. "Mom"—my voice struggled—"can I please just get my things?"

She didn't speak. Only nodded her head *yes*, and opened the door just wide enough for me and Caleb to walk through. I let go of my son's hand as soon as we crossed the threshold, grateful to be out of the December cold and for the chance to run upstairs and pack my possessions as quickly as I could. Caleb stayed downstairs with his grandmother during the half hour that it took me to stuff all the essential items inside my suitcases. Veronica said nothing to me from the time I entered her house to the time I finally left it.

• • •

It was the middle of December 2003 when Caleb and I moved in with Mateo. But by the beginning of the new year, I was beginning to find life almost unbearable. Mateo cooked and cleaned, and he made love to me...whenever he was around. But most of the time he was gone...with *my* car. And sometimes his cousin Travis would sleep over. But I needed the attention Mateo gave me, whenever he gave it to me, and I thought that if I gave him everything he needed, he would eventually love me back.

Things were isolated for me and Caleb. The only reprieve we got was when I went to work on the weekends and he went to his grandmother's to be baby-sat. For two days out of the week, we could finally *breathe*.

By the end of February, things started to look up when Mateo finally found a new job—an apprenticeship position with the Ironworkers, for which he was getting paid fairly well. Surprisingly, though, nothing changed for us. And now that he was working every day, I had to either take him to work, or let him take *me* to work so he could keep my car. The court had dismissed his pending assault and possession charges because of the injuries he received from the arresting officer, *not* the other way around. As a result, however, Mateo did give up selling drugs. But he never wanted any bills in his name and therefore, didn't believe in having a car note. He wanted to save his money and *buy* a used car straight out. His way of thinking made no sense to me, but I still believed I could make him do right one day, if I hung in there long enough.

I found out I was pregnant towards the beginning of March. Despite the situation and the obvious differences in morals and ethics between me and Mateo, I was incredibly elated that I would finally be tied to him forever. Even though I knew it was wrong, I didn't care. And the thing is, once you think you've reached a limit to the choices that are available to you, you start accepting things that

93

are well below standard, falling for anything and *everything* as you slowly begin to forget who you once were, what you once stood for.

9

Too Far Gone

If I squeezed my eyes tight enough, I could make myself believe anything I wanted to...

As I drove home to Mateo's apartment one afternoon, I thought about Ian and wondered what he was doing in New Jersey. Was he happy? Did he love his new job? Did he ever think of me? Why did he leave me behind...? My mind traveled back to the evening he picked me up from the apartment and took me out for dinner. We held hands in the middle of his car's console, and I fell in love with him all over again as I stole glances of him navigating the steering wheel with just one, steady hand—the same expert steadiness he used to maneuver my developing sexuality while loving me.

I was a few weeks pregnant then. But soon after we had placed our orders, a severe bout of morning sickness took over, and we had to take our food to go.

That was right before we decided on the abortion. And ever since I moved in with Mateo, I found myself often wondering how life would have turned out if I had kept our child.

I didn't love Mateo, but since I didn't even love myself, I didn't realize this fact almost twenty years ago. I had been living with him for almost two months, but I was almost beginning to miss living with my mother. Maybe if I had just learned to ignore her jabs at my character and turn away from her regular vicious looks and just suck it up, I wouldn't have felt the need to seek solace at Mateo's for a whole weekend... and *she* wouldn't have had the chance to change the locks on me.

But I was too far gone. Stuck in a mire of mind control and confusion about who was worse—Mateo or Veronica? And between the two of them, I just knew I was going to wind up blowing my brains out trying to please one or the other.

When I finally pulled up to the apartment complex, I shook my head forcefully as if I could permanently erase my memories of Ian, and reluctantly brought myself back to the present so that I could safely park the car. I was almost eight weeks pregnant with Mateo's first child, so I had no choice but to leave Ian where he'd left me and move forward. I was miserable, but would never admit this out loud. I still survived on the belief that Mateo and I had a chance, even though I knew deep down that we didn't. I now recognized that he only invited me to move in with him because he had lost his job and needed my help with his rent. What a fool I was! I wasn't even his *type,* and let's call a spade a spade—he wasn't even *my* type. But what else was I supposed to do? What else *could* I do? Leave and go *where*? I worked twelve-hour shifts—who else was going to help me take care of Caleb after the daycare closed at 6 p.m.? Mateo and I fed off each other. He needed me for my stability, and I needed him for whatever I tried to fool myself into thinking he could give me. And that was enough for me.

After climbing the two flights of steps to Mateo's apartment, I saw a folded piece of paper stuck inside the dark tan door. It was from the rental office. As soon as I let myself in, I opened the note and began reading. Apparently, we were behind in our rent for February; plus, we owed almost $150 in late fees. I figured it had to be a mistake, knowing I had given Mateo $800 to cover the rent that he didn't have at the very beginning of the month. I must've read the notice five times before deciding to give the leasing office a call. My name wasn't on the lease, so I wasn't sure they'd give me any information, but that was *my* money that had suddenly come up missing.

The leasing office phone rang once before a woman answered on the other end.

"Maple Court Apartments...this is Eva..can I help you?"

"Um, hi, Eva. This is Megan in apartment 4007, number 412. I got a notice saying that the rent was not paid for this month...?"

I heard a shuffle of some papers on the other end before she kindly asked if she could place me on hold. When she got back to the line after two minutes, she cleared everything up for me.

"Um, yes. Mateo James is behind by fifteen days. We've filed court fees in the amount of $150, and he's due in court on the 20th of this month."

I sucked in my breath, thoroughly confused. "So it wasn't paid for this month?"

"No, ma'am," she said, ever so nicely. "But if you get us the money by Friday, we'll consider the account up to date, and he won't have to go to court."

I told her thank you and hung up the phone. After taking off my shoes, I moved into the bedroom and sat on the bed, wondering what to do next.

I hadn't moved from Mateo's bed by the time he got home from work an hour later. The notice from the rental office still remained in my sweaty palm when he entered the bedroom. He looked at me, and I thought I saw a flitter of guilt cross his face.

"What's wrong?" he asked slowly, watching me carefully.

My pregnancy hormones raging since first reading about our late balance, I slowly stood, walked up to him, and shoved the white paper towards his chest.

"What the hell is *this*, Mateo?"

It took him no time to match my anger, and he snatched the paper from me. As he read it, he pretended to be surprised, as if he had no idea how $800 magically missed the hands of the leasing personnel.

"Megan...I...I'll get the money back so I can pay for this—"

"—and what the fuck did you do with my money, Mateo?" I had raised my voice, my eyes centered angrily on him. I had never shown him my temper before—in fact, I was never ever even aware of any temper I had before meeting Mateo—but that $800 was a huge chunk of my tax refund.

"Megan. Sit down, and stop screaming at me. Let me explain what I did..."

"That was *my* money, Mateo! *My money!*"

He moved closer to me, and I was forced back onto the bed, as his 150 pounds easily outweighed me. "I used the money you gave me to try and buy a pound and flip it..."

Flip it? What the hell was he talking about?

"What the *fuck* are you talking about??"

"Megan, I bought a pound of weed—"

"—you bought just a pound of weed for *$800*, Mateo—?"

"Yes, *Megan.*" He looked up towards the ceiling and blew out a frustrated breath before looking back at me. *Frustrated for what? It wasn't like it was his money that was practically stolen.* "I bought a pound of *weed* and thought I could double my money to better help us out..."

The insides of my head began swirling as I wondered what the hell I had gotten myself into when I moved in with Mateo. Suddenly, my eyes spotted some twenty-dollar bills poking out of his jeans pocket, and without thinking, the adrenaline pumping through my blood gave me the courage to lunge at his waist and pull the stack of money out of his pocket. It must've been at least $300.

"This is MY money!" I screamed. And just as quickly, Mateo grabbed my right wrist, twisted it ninety degrees, and took his money back. I dropped to the floor in pain.

"Bitch, don't *ever* touch my money, you hear me? This is *my* shit!"

He still had my wrist, so I kicked his shin. Instantly, he kicked me in my left thigh. I was stunned and yelled out in pain. My own father had never even hit me. Realizing what he had done, Mateo then let go of my wrist and knelt to the floor beside me. I shouted at him, "I was nice enough to help you with the money you needed! I don't have that kind of money to just throw away, *Mateo*!"

"Megan...I'm sorry..." He stopped to catch his breath. "I didn't mean to. Get up, baby."

"Fuck you," I spat. His mood changed abruptly again as he glared at me through eyes that seemed to darken right before me as his hands began to twitch, as if he were trying to control himself from grabbing me again.

He got up and left me there. I waited on the carpeted floor for about five minutes until I heard him open and close the front door. I waited for a second longer before I gathered myself together and made a phone call to Kelly, one of the few friends I had left since having Caleb four years before. She instructed me to get my belongings and go to her house immediately.

I did as I was told. Heart beating unsteadily, I gathered my and

Caleb's things as fast as I could and ran to my car. Breathing hard, I thought about what just happened. Even though Mateo's temper was short, he had never put his hands on me before that day—all because of some fucking money...*my money*. As I waited for my Nissan to warm up, I inspected the red marks making bracelets around my wrist. I knew I didn't deserve what just happened, but I was too far in it now to do anything about it. I had already tricked myself into believing that I loved Mateo with almost every inch of my being—I would have walked to the ends of the earth and back again if he asked me to. The spell he had over me was *unimaginable*. And being pregnant with his first child now made his grip on me permanent.

• • •

Kelly lived just over the Woodrow Wilson Bridge, in Arlington, Virginia, about 30 minutes from Temple Hills. When I knocked on her door, with my heart still thudding against my ribcage, she promptly answered it and immediately pulled me close to her and let me cry into her arms.

"Megan, you're gonna stay here and find another place for you and Caleb. You are *not* gonna go back to Mateo. Do you understand me?"

I muffled my cries and pulled from her embrace to look at her. "You'd do that for me?"

She took my hand. "Of course. I have this whole place to myself, and Philip is the only one who comes over on a regular basis. He won't mind."

She then leaned in closer to me and spoke gently but firmly. "And you're gonna end this pregnancy, as well..."

I felt my eyes grow huge and I quickly withdrew my hand from her grasp. "You mean...I should have an abortion...? Kelly, I can't do that." But she shook her head back and forth at me, keeping her stance. I continued to watch her stern eyes and I finally backed down, defeated.

She took my hand in hers once more. "Megan, honey, listen to me. I'm not trying to judge you, but I just need you to see that you have Caleb—how in the world are you going to be able to cope with another one? Mateo isn't the right one for you, and because of this, there's no sense in making matters worse—for you, for Caleb, *and* for a new baby. Think about it."

I let out a puff of air and momentarily closed my eyes. What she was saying made perfect sense. But nothing I did or thought had made any sense since my first abortion seven years ago. My sins only became greater and my thought processes only grew more obscure as my mind steadily surrendered to the vortex that continued to devour whatever was left of any sound judgment I might have once had.

She continued to watch me with her sharp green eyes, quietly driving home the point she just expressed through her stare. Once satisfied her message was clearly received, she extended her hand and rubbed my arm. "Now come on in and have a seat while I make you a cup of tea."

• • •

Two days after I had shown up at Kelly's apartment like an orphaned cat, I scheduled myself to get the abortion with a local reproductive clinic, *again*.

I was now in the shower. Kelly was in her bedroom, sleeping after her night shift at the hospital, and Caleb was in the living room playing with a hand-held game system. I was trying hard to calm down inside the hot stream of water directed at my face, but the anxiety was like a clutch around my throat. It was hard to breathe, hard to swallow, and I imagined myself going to sleep and never waking up because it was impossible for me to come up with any solutions that didn't include another *abortion*.

I forced open my eyes and located the natural rosehip and vanilla bath wash Kelly kept inside her shower. I smiled. I loved her shower. It was big, but warm and cozy. It had this window to the upper left that looked out to nothing but sunny skies and trees. There was also this huge metal shower caddy that extended from floor to ceiling, holding everything from different scented soaps to different varieties of shaving gels. I loved the whole set-up and couldn't wait until I could do this for my own apartment someday.

I sighed, suddenly thinking of Mateo and the apartment we had shared for less than six months. I hated that place, actually. It was situated in the less-than desirable parts of Temple Hills, and it didn't have a huge shower with a window that let the promising skies in. My eyes began to tear up. I had no idea what I was going to do. Even though I was set to terminate the pregnancy the following week, I couldn't imagine cutting off ties with Mateo James forever.

After showering, I stepped outside the shower and viewed myself in the bathroom mirror. I was shocked to see that I had already gained a couple of pounds in my belly and my breasts were already swelling. I didn't know why I hadn't noticed them before today. I gently took both full breasts in my hands, slightly cupping them to make sure that what I saw was real. I then shook my head at my reflection and decided I couldn't go ahead with another abortion, seeing that my breasts were already starting to fill to accommodate the tiny little baby inside me. I would keep the pregnancy and deal with the consequences later.

I massaged my skin with Kelly's expensive vanilla cream and pulled on my clean clothes. After leaving the bathroom, I went into the living room and quietly canceled my appointment with the family planning clinic, making sure Kelly wouldn't overhear me.

I then made an appointment to see an apartment later that day, back in Maryland, not too far from where I had lived when I was with Ian. The rent was $720/month, all utilities included. It was perfect for me and Caleb.

"Whatcha doing?"

"Omigod!" I quickly turned around and faced Kelly. She had a big grin across her face as she watched me, apparently very amused that she was able to startle my thoughts. I folded my cell phone shut and returned her smile. "You scared me!"

"Ahhhh, I'm sorry." She embraced me and rubbed my back. "Looking for a new place?"

I let her go and stood back, admiring her. Kelly was cute— she had light blonde curls that fell just over her shoulders, a super skinny figure, and that *black girl ass* that Mateo always teased me about *not* having. I often wondered why she would want anything to do with me, considering the shit I always managed to get myself into. She had her college education, parents who supported her, and a nice ass apartment in Arlington, a suburb of D.C. that made tiny little Temple Hills, Maryland look like the most desolate place in all of the world. God, I wanted what Kelly had. I even wanted what *Veronica* had. Why did I have to go and keep fucking up? And see, I *knew* I was fucking up, but I just couldn't *stop fucking up.*

I took one of Kelly's curls into my hand and smiled. "Yes, I'm going to go look at this place back in Hyattsville, where I used to live."

She smiled back. "Good. Somewhere far away from that Mateo asshole."

I flinched at her words, but said nothing.

Kelly didn't seem to notice. "What time do you have to be

103

there?"

I looked at my phone. "Three p.m." It was nearing two now. "I'd better get ready to go. Do you mind if Caleb stays here with you? I'll just be gone for about an hour and a half, tops."

"Sure. No problem. And then when you get back, we can all go out to dinner, my treat."

I tried my best to keep the plastic smile glued to my face—the smile that proved to Kelly that I was in agreement with everything she said about Mateo and my need to move on and never look back. The same smile that masked the tortuous struggle presently happening between my heart and mind, and their need to finally align with one another. I nodded my head towards my friend. "Cool. Thanks. I'll be back as soon as I can." I rushed off, but the anxiety quickened my heartbeat once again because even though I understood I was doing the right thing by getting my own apartment, I had to *force myself* to do it. Mateo hit me, he *stole* from me, he never called to say he was sorry or to check on me since I left. And yet, I was *still* emotionally fixed, so what did that ultimately say about who I was as a woman and as a mother?

Unfortunately, I couldn't even tell you.

10

Back In

He called me six weeks after Caleb and I had settled in our new apartment. I was surprised I was able to just...stop...and play make-believe... as if Mateo had never existed for as long as I did. He asked me about the growing baby inside of me, but seemed completely shocked when he realized I had been able to get my own place, complete with my new babysitter -turned- friend, Constance, who was able to watch Caleb the three days I worked at the hospital.

I let him back in the day after he called. Had to hold my head high and keep my breathing steady so that I wouldn't let on that I was *over-the-moon* ecstatic that he was back in my presence.

"Hey." I spoke softly when I opened my door and looked up at him with huge, innocent, and hopeful brown eyes. I had braided my hair the night before so that it would fall around my face in loose waves once I undid the plaits that morning.

I watched him as he looked from my face down to my belly. "What's up? You alright?"

I gave him a smile. "Yeah, I'm ok. Just *really* nauseous. This morning sickness is no joke." I turned my face away from him and took in a deep breath as the scent of his *Dove* soap bar began making the nausea even worse. Then I moved out of the way and made room for him to enter. "You can come in. But, shoes off please."

He gave me a look that said, *You're really gonna tell me what to do?* But this was *my* place and I wasn't budging. After pushing his sneakers from his feet and leaving them haphazardly at the door, he cautiously walked further inside and checked out his surroundings. There was a living room/dining room immediately to the right of the entrance, a small kitchen to the left, a short hallway with a linen closet, and a bedroom towards the back.

"It's nothing big or anything, but it's what I can afford."

He stopped and looked at me again, taking a minute or two to study my thicker hair and growing belly. I tried not to look into his dark eyes again, but after a second of awkward silence inside that still apartment, I relented...and took my drug again.

• • •

Mateo began staying with me not even two weeks after he had first visited my newly-found independence. His first assignment with the Ironworkers had him working in Greenbelt, which was located only five minutes down the street from my apartment. He spent his nights with me Sunday through Thursday while I spent my mornings *and afternoons* taking him to work and picking him up. And when that got too exhausting for my pregnant body, I just let him take my car. By the time Friday rolled around, he'd take me to work before the sun even *thought* about rising for the day, and after my 12-hour shift I'd have to wait for him to come pick me up in *my* car. Then he'd be off for the weekends, and Caleb and I would be on our own again. Thank God for Constance, who lived in the same apartment complex as me...who had become a truly, faithful friend.

It didn't take me long to realize Mateo was using me (again). I felt it every time he took my car to work without even a second thought as to what Caleb and I had going on for the day. Felt it, also, when he fucked me *hard,* knowing I had a human inside of me, only there to enjoy the experience of *not* having to worry about protection since we were already way beyond that. He didn't help me with the rent, the car note, or the gas needed to use my car. He never cooked or cleaned. I was still on my own, even though his body was there, using me at his leisure, as always. Caleb didn't like him there, either. Not that he said as much, but it was evident in his sudden habit of staying silent whenever Mateo was around; his voice was only a whisper towards me when he *absolutely needed* to speak—you could even almost see Caleb visibly *shake* in Mateo's angry presence. I was a shitty-ass mother as I watched my son begin to slowly succumb to the same anxiety I suffered from, not even realizing it back then because I was so focused on Mateo. Caleb and I had made great strides in finding our own place, and now I was back to fucking up again by letting a man back in, when he had *no right* to be there. But as long as he was there, that was all that I needed. My progress, Caleb's stability, and my emotional *in*stability meant absolutely nothing when it came to Mateo James.

• • •

I looked over at Caleb from my place at the kitchen table. He was fast asleep on our air mattress in the living room, but I was worried about him. He had thrown up twice an hour ago, and also had diarrhea. The poo was so bad, I ended up having to put a *Pull-up* on him, just in case, even though he was almost five-years-old.

It was 8 p.m. and Mateo wasn't home. Funny—his shift ended at 3 everyday. And he still didn't have a cell for me to call him on. But he had my car.

At 10, he finally showed. Didn't say much to me. Didn't offer any apology or any explanation. Just showered and took his ass to bed...*my* bed. Any other day, I would've wanted to gouge his eyes out, but that night I was too worried about my son to say anything.

At around 11, I heard Caleb trying to throw-up again from my spot in the bedroom. I jumped out of bed to help him, but there was no food or bile coming up, only acid. He kept dry heaving, while at the same time, soiling his diaper. I got so scared that I called the nurse's advice line, and was told to take him to the ER in case he was becoming dehydrated. I threw on some clothes and tried my best to dress Caleb. I then went to the bedroom to wake Mateo. For some reason, I was scared of his reaction.

He was pissed that I had awakened him, and he insisted that Caleb was going to be okay, that I was just overreacting. I hated him for that.

I spoke carefully, though, because I was nervous. I hated him, but I was also *scared* of him. "Well, I know you have to get to work in the morning, and I don't know how long we'll be in the hospital...sooooo....so maybe I'll just take a taxi to the hospital and I'll leave the car here with you..." I waited for a response, praying that he wouldn't allow me to call for a taxi when I had my car just outside the apartment.

But all he did was roll over, face the opposite side, and mumble, "Alright, thanks."

God, what was I doing?

• • •

The nurses and doctors at the nearby hospital ended up giving Caleb an IV to rehydrate him. Once he received some intravenous nausea medicine, he felt a lot better. He was finally released at 6 in the morning. I was exhausted, but thankful that his vomiting had stopped.

We took a cab back home that morning. Mateo had already left for work. *Fucking bastard.* But I only had myself to blame because I continued to take his shit. Continued to take it because that *bastard* was my lifeline.

· · ·

"You know we're wasting money paying for two apartments, right?"

I didn't know what he was talking about because he *definitely* wasn't shelling out any money for *my* place. But Mateo was my drug, and wherever he wanted to take me, even if it was to the depths of Hell, I followed.

It wasn't that hard for Mateo to convince me to give up any progress I had made since moving into my apartment. First of all, we didn't have central air. I would have to buy my own AC unit and hang it inside one of the windows, and *then get charged* extra for each unit I kept during the summer months. Then, there was that incident when I was sitting inside my car one day, trying to catch my breath before turning the engine off. Out of nowhere, the property manager appeared, and with a tap on my car's window, told me that I could no longer park in my assigned parking space near my building. According to him, there was some insane rule that said residents couldn't sit in their cars for more than five minutes, due to the possibility of them selling or buying drugs.

???

So now I had to find street parking when I got home—with my swollen feet, Caleb in tow, and groceries if I were coming from the store.

I drew in a huge breath. "I guess you're right—"

"—I mean, we could just move into your place—it doesn't

matter to me. I just think that this apartment got way too much bullshit going on for the amount of rent you're paying..."

It *did* matter to him; he couldn't fool me there. I knew he missed his home; plus, his father had rented the apartment for him so I knew he wasn't going to give it up.

I let my breath leave my body slowly. "Your apartment it is." But I should've just stayed in mine...sucked up all the bullshit ass rules that *Ager Station Apartments* came with...saved and bought a window unit...and found a way to kick Mateo out of my life. I should have just done everything I could to get back to the peace I had successfully established for me and Caleb *before* I opened the door again for Mateo. My need for others ran so deep that it never mattered how badly they treated me. All that mattered was that somebody was *there.*

• • •

The abuse continued after I returned to Maple Court Apartments, even though Mateo promised me that he would never hit me again. But I would soon realize that once abuse starts, it rarely ever ends. And that's the God-honest truth. No matter how hard I cried, no matter how much I begged, no matter how much pain I suffered, Mateo was too angry with himself to stop. And surprisingly, I *knew* at this point that it wasn't me. My brain had actually maintained enough rationale to know that Mateo's fury had nothing to do with me. I mean, how could it? I was faithful, resourceful, and waited on Mateo hand and foot while pushing my needs further down on the *to-do* list as the months dragged on.

The only thing left to do was to tell Mateo one last time to *fuck off*, take my car back, and drive off into the sunset with Caleb strapped securely in his booster seat. *Yeah, right.* Even though I had a modicum of logic still left inside me, I was without the *courage* needed to ride off to greener pastures.

Mateo and I would be good for a week, and then the arguments would start all over again, as if there were an alarm set to sound off regularly. I didn't know why he hated me and Caleb so much. Mostly, we fought about his staying out too late, especially after the one- hundredth time that I heard his key turn the door's lock after 3 a.m. I could've *sworn* he was sleeping with someone else, but he always insisted that he was just "hustling" in Southeast... even though he had given up his silly little drug trade months before. If he had gone back to selling drugs, however, why did we always come up short for money? Why was I even paying half the rent? Why was there never any money for me to buy an outfit for Caleb, or to even treat myself to a pedicure every now and then? If he were *hustling* as he said he was, he was doing a damn poor job of it.

But he was my drug of choice. Not too many side effects: just the occasional crying from all the yelling and screaming, as well as the occasional feelings of low self-worth...and maybe here and there, absentminded drifts into another world, far away from my pathetic reality, as I struggled to remember who I was before I decided to abuse this drug. But just as an addict does, I continued to reassure myself that everything was going to be just swell. And when the aftermath settled once again, I looked forward to the high that this drug gave me, relishing in the temporary façade of love that I received, right before the side effects took hold of my mind once again.

11

The Cycle

Mateo and I were back at it because he didn't come home until the sun began to make her ascension through the morning sky. I had been up the entire night, worried that I wouldn't be able to get to work on time because he also had my car. So when Mateo decided to finally show his face at the apartment at 6 a.m., I immediately began screaming about how it wasn't right for him to leave me in the house, pregnant, all night...how he got to playfully roam the streets all night in *my car*...and about how it was *fucked up* for him to complain about how I never cooked a good meal every day, and yet on the days that I did, he was never around to eat it, anyway. We were arguing at six in the fucking morning, and I had to be at work in a fucking hour.

We both shouted and hollered at one another, until he smacked me in the side of my face, knocking me to the carpet.

"Get the fuck outta my place!"

"NO!" My voice had quickly become a hoarse whisper. My right ear started to ring loudly and I began seeing purple and pink stars shimmer in front of my eyes. I clamped my hand over my injured ear, and looked up at my opponent. I started to beg while the tears poured without my permission. "I have to take a shower,

Mateo, and get to work!"

"*What*? " His black face twisted into something awful before he scoffed at me. "This is *my* fucking apartment, so get your shit and go!"

I stared at him with my mouth hung open, not believing he was actually serious, until he grabbed my shoulders, forced me to a standing position, and ushered me out of the apartment like I was his prisoner. I had just enough time to grab my bag and my cell phone before he pushed me through the open door, and slammed it behind me.

I looked through blinding tears at my cell phone. It was now 6:20 a.m. I sniffled and rubbed the hurt side of my face. My drug had worn off around one in the morning, when I awakened and realized that Mateo wasn't under the blankets with me. I unfolded my cell, headed down the stairs to my car, let myself into the Nissan, and locked the door to make sure I was safe before dialing 911. I told them that my boyfriend had thrown me out of the house where I helped to pay rent, and that I just needed to grab my scrubs so I could get to work. I sat in my car and waited for the police, and wondered what I was going to do next. Thank God Caleb was with my mother for the weekend.

I stayed in my car, keeping my eyes on the apartment, hoping that Mateo would leave and that the police would hurry up and rescue me. Ten minutes later, Prince George's County's finest arrived and convinced Mateo to let me back into the apartment. He was gone by the time I exited my car and traveled the two flights of stairs to the apartment. Two policemen stood by and kept their eyes on me while I hurried and grabbed my uniform and clogs.

I left the apartment with my scrubs and shoes with the intention of changing discreetly inside my car. The police let me move past them first, out of the apartment, before closing the door behind them. But they weren't able to lock it, and neither was I, because that bastard had taken my house keys before he left. I traveled back down the steps and did a quick search for any sign of Mateo. When I decided he was gone, I got back into my car, turned the ignition, pulled my scrubs on over my night clothes, and began my drive to work. But it wasn't until I had driven two miles down Branch Avenue when I decided that I couldn't go to work. Not with the purple and pink stars still floating, mockingly, in front of my eyes...not with the apartment door still left unlocked...and not without having a surefire way of being able to get back into the damn place, since I now had no key. I pulled over to the right at an Exxon gas station and called my job. It was now 6:50 a.m., entirely *way* too late to call out and find someone to replace me in the next 10 minutes, but I wasn't going to work like this.

"Hello. 2 Bles. May I help you?"

I nervously pulled the loose hair back from the right side of my head and secured the strands behind my ear. I took a breath and forced some tears from my eyes. "Hi, this is Megan. May I please speak with the charge nurse?"

"Um, yes...hold on. Wait a minute—Megan? Is this Megan?" It was then that I recognized the voice of Charlotte, one of the nurses on the oncology unit that I had worked on as a technician for the past year and some months.

"Um, yes, it's me—"

"—are you ok?" Charlotte sounded genuinely concerned.

"No," I said through the tears that now fell freely over my cheeks. "I was in a car accident, and I can't make it to work today." I felt horrible for lying, but I wouldn't dare tell them that I couldn't make it because my *boyfriend* hit me and then took the house keys from me.

"Oh, ok, ok." Charlotte sounded rushed, but still concerned.

"Let me get Rebecca for you. I hope you feel better!"

I sniffled through the phone, just to make my story sound more believable, starting to feel like a real jerk. "Okay. Thanks, Charlotte."

• • •

I then called the nurse advice line to see if I could get an appointment to make sure that my ear was okay from earlier; I also wanted to get a doctor's note to cover me from my inconsiderately late call-out. The nurse on the other end of the phone scheduled an appointment with my OBGYN within the hour. Since the doctor was only ten minutes from where I was now, I could see her real quickly, and then head back to *Mateo's* apartment before he had a chance to get back home from work and lock the door on me.

• • •

The apartment door was still unlocked and the place was just how I had left it when I grabbed my clothes four hours before. The baby growing inside me was okay, and my ear and head just needed to be iced. I left the doctor's office with a note excusing me from work for the day, and a small rectangular card that listed the numbers to agencies that were available to help victims of domestic abuse.

Wow. I smirked to myself as I studied the card for a second time since receiving it, then stuffed it inside my handbag.

After checking the two bedrooms and the bathroom to make sure I was alone in the place, I plopped down inside of the comfortable armchair that was next to the sliding glass door. I directed my gaze to the outside world and thought about Adam.

I met Adam Hartley six years ago through the crafty Cheyanne. Even though Cheyanne was a junior at Elizabeth

Seton High School and I was a senior, we were taking the same Drawing & Painting class.

"Guess what, chica?"

"What?" I paused my search for graduation dresses and met Cheyanne's sly grin. "You look like you're up to something..."

"I've got someone who wants to meet you—"

"—ohhh, noooo, not this again, Cheyanne. I told you—I can't. Not now. You forget Veronica is putting me on the plane back to my father's first thing next week?"

I kept my eyes on Cheyanne as her round olive face reddened some, while her mischievous black eyes sparkled. "He's twenty-two...in the military...and he liked what he saw—"

"—liked what he saw *when*?"

She gave a chuckle. "When I showed him your picture, *girl*!"

I shook my head in confusion. "*What picture*, Cheyanne? And no, he's way too old. I'm barely eighteen."

Cheyanne pursed her lips and shook her head once more. "He's not too old, Megan. *God*, you're such a goody-two-shoes! I showed him your graduation pictures, and he fell in love. Maybe you need someone a little more mature than you." She turned her attention to the dress rack and carefully lifted a white dress. "Here, how 'bout this? You're taking entirely too long to pick out a simple white dress; we've got other things to do."

• • •

I jumped suddenly, and moved my eyes from the glass door to my round belly, remembering that there was a human being inside of me. As I felt another foot (or a hand) attempt to push through my skin, I smiled. But the joy was short-lived as I remembered the card that was kindly given to me by my doctor, barely an hour before.

I was a battered woman, and I continued to live as one because 1) I was pregnant with Mateo's child; 2) Mateo was the only "father figure" Caleb knew since Adam had successfully evaporated from the face of the earth; and 3) I thought that if I continued to love Mateo hard enough, he would change. He would realize how good I was to him and how much I unconditionally loved him, and he would finally find the desire to change into a better man.

Unicorns and fairy dust.

I missed Ian.

• • •

I heard the ringing inside of my ear again and lifted my hand to carefully touch it, being painfully reminded of the encounter with Mateo earlier that morning, as well as all of the other altercations that were now a regular part of our year-long relationship. To be perfectly honest, though, I wasn't sure anymore if I even loved Mateo. Maybe it was just a simple matter of my welding myself to him because I didn't have Adam in my life anymore, or anyone else for that matter. And I *hated*, more than anything in this world, to be alone.

I used him just as he used me.

The only good thing between Mateo and me was the life that was growing quickly inside of my womb. I was sure Mateo looked forward to the day his son was born, but was absolutely convinced on most days that he *hated* me.

I was almost sure of the love Adam had for me, too, until he left me high and dry when I told him I was pregnant with Caleb.

I began to wonder that if Adam had never disappeared, would I have still fallen so deep into this mess that Mateo and I continued to create?

• • •

Four hours later, I heard keys jingle inside the lock of the front door, and, as if on cue, my heart instantly started to pound as I waited for Mateo to finally push the door open. I sat in frightened silence and stared at him as he stepped inside the apartment. He looked at me in surprise for a second, then dropped his hard hat at the front door and rushed over to me. I watched, amazed, as he knelt down onto the floor at my knees and began speaking briskly.

"What are you doing home from work? What's wrong? Are you okay? I'm so sorry..." He wrapped his arms around me and looked up at me. I began to cry. It was time for me to take my drug again. I started to explain myself through tears. *God,* I was getting so sick and tired of the tears.

"I tried to go to work, but I couldn't, because I didn't know if I had a home to come back to. I was scared you were gonna lock me out for good, so I came back home. I didn't even go to work..." I was crying and blubbering, and I was so relieved that we weren't fighting any longer.

"But I told you that you didn't have to go back to work anymore, baby. I told you I would take care of you..."

I paused—he'd never told me he'd take care of me.

I knew I shouldn't believe him, though, not when he so easily threw me out of his house less than eight hours before. But with a baby on the way, what else was I supposed to do? I had allowed myself to become trapped again by moving back in with Mateo, and at this point, unless I went to a shelter, there was no way out of this.

I stared deep into his eyes, my own eyes begging for his empathy, and continued to cry burning tears. *Why couldn't we just fix this?!?* I was at a loss for what to do because I didn't understand what he wanted from me! If I were trying so hard to make sure he had what he needed, to make sure he was happy, why was he so mean to me? I wanted to ask him, but I was exhausted; instead, I stayed quiet as he gathered me in his arms, carried me to the bedroom that we shared, and made love to me. I took my drug and everything was going to be alright again.

12

Little Lamb

I was out of work on medical leave by the beginning of August. At my 20th week of gestation, I had to have an emergency cerclage placed because I had begun dilating way before the baby's due date. Being off from work kind of excited me, however, because I was able to spend more time with Caleb. It would also give me the time to (hopefully) get my life back together before I made it back to work in the next couple of months. Mateo and I were also doing a little better as a couple.

• • •

"Mommy, where are we going?"

Caleb and I were on the freeway, heading north towards Baltimore. It was a hot day outside, but it was nice enough for Caleb as we headed towards Target. I was looking forward to the birth of our baby boy, and I needed to price some cribs and buy at least a handful of jumpsuits, some warm socks, and a couple of packs of diapers for him.

I took a quick look at Caleb and smiled at him. "We're going to the store so we can pick out some baby things. I'm gonna need your help, ok?"

"Sure, mommy. No problem."

Just then, my cell phone rang. Keeping my eyes on the road, I fished it out of my purse and carefully flipped it open. "Hello?"

"What's up?"

My heart ballooned. It was Mateo. Since being home from work, he was now making it a habit of using his coworker's cell phone to call me to make sure I was doing ok. My smile grew brighter. "Hey! We're out here, on our way to Target to get some stuff for the baby—"

"*Target?*" He jokingly said it like he thought it was the most repulsive store on the planet.

"Yes, *Target.*" I laughed. "Do you need anything?"

"Nah, I'm good. Where's Caleb?"

I really appreciated his concern. "He's with me. I'll be back in time to get you from work."

"Alright. Just make sure you're drinking enough water. It's hot as shit out here."

I was in heaven, loving all the concern he seemed to have for me lately. My drug was now working longer than usual. "Yep! Got my water bottle right here with me. I'll see you in a few."

We hung up and I felt like everything was finally going to be okay.

After I picked Mateo up from work and babbled on and on about the baby items I had picked up, I started to feel sick, like I was coming down with the flu, but just figured that being out in the heat had something to do with it. By that evening, around 6 p.m., I began having contractions, which were coming closer and closer together as the hour grew nearer to seven. I thought they were just Braxton-Hicks contractions...until they started coming every five minutes. I was due in November, though, so Mateo and

I decided to go to the hospital.

We packed up Caleb's belongings and left him with Mateo's grandmother and his Aunt Alicia, who lived twenty minutes down the street, in the District. They seemed happy to take him. Ten minutes later, we arrived at the hospital, where I was triaged and immediately hooked up to an IV drip of magnesium to stop the contractions.

No one knew why I was having the constant contractions, but they eventually stopped after two hours, and I was released. Something inside of me urged me that I should've been admitted, but the doctors assured me that since my amniotic sac had not opened and my cervix had not dilated any further than it already had previously, I was fine to go home and be on *strict* bed rest for the next couple of days. So Mateo took me home.

• • •

It was around 3 p.m. the next day when I awoke from a nap. Caleb had gone to the neighbor's house to play about two hours before, and since the apartment had been quiet and I had been exhausted, I decided to take advantage of an empty place. Mateo was still at work. Even though I had been sleeping for almost two hours, I woke up feeling spent...and cold, like the life force was quickly draining from me. I struggled to sit up and go to the bathroom to find the thermometer to take my temperature. After putting the digital piece under my tongue, I waited thirty seconds before it read 104.3.

"Hmmm..," I mumbled to myself. I powered it off and ran it under hot water and laid it on the sink to air-dry. I glimpsed at the mirror and into my bloodshot eyes. I felt my belly. I could feel my baby boy moving inside me, but I wasn't having any more contractions. Turning off the light, I trudged heavily back to the sofa and reached for the phone. I was going to call Kelly, but figured she was probably at work. I turned the phone on and pushed the numbers for the nurse advice line. After punching in my medical ID number and waiting a few seconds for the advice nurse to come on the line, I told her how I was feeling.

"...yes, and my temp is 104.3..." I started fanning myself with a sheet of paper. Now I was turning hot.

"And how many months are you, Ms. Harris?"

"I'm six months."

"Okay. And you've felt the baby move within the past hour?"

"Yes. But I'm not having any contractions. I was just in the hospital last night for contractions, but they've since stopped..."

She interrupted me. "You were in the hospital *last night*?"

I closed my eyes and began to rub my left temple with my free hand. This woman was asking me too many questions, and second by second was feeling like my life was quickly leaving. "Yes...last night."

"Oookayyy," the nurse blew slowly and carefully. "I'm gonna need you to please go to the emergency room as soon as you can, okay?"

My eyes popped open, and I stopped rubbing my head. My heavy eyes traveled to the wall clock hanging over the dining room table. It was 3:15 p.m., and Mateo wasn't home yet and he didn't have a cell phone for me to call him. And he had my car...

I told myself to calm down, that it was going to be just fine. "Yes, I will go right away to the hospital."

"Okay. You get to the hospital as soon as you can and if anything changes between now and then, please call the our advice nurse line, alright?"

I swallowed a small lump that had begun to grow deep in my throat. I wanted to cry. "Okay," I mumbled.

"And good luck to you, Ms. Harris."

I clicked the phone off and got back up, forcing myself into the bedroom that Mateo and I shared. It was hot outside, and my pregnant body couldn't take anymore of the heat. I pulled on the lightest thing that I had to wear, a pair of light pink, cotton gym shorts, and a white tee. I slipped my swollen feet into a pair of pink flip flops and walked carefully back to the sofa. I was going to wait ten more minutes for Mateo to come home, and if not, I was going to go to the hospital by ambulance.

• • •

"Megan. Megan? Megan, wake up."

I slowly opened my eyes and looked at the person who was shaking my arm. After my eyes adjusted I was able to see that it was Mateo. I moved my head a little and looked at the wall clock. "Wait, it's only 3:45—what are you doing home so early?" I felt a strange wetness across my forehead. I wiped at it—it was a mess of hair and sweat. But that movement alone took too much effort, so I relaxed against the pillows of the sofa and let my eyes close–

"Megan...Megan, what's wrong? Open your eyes, baby."

I felt my eyeballs move beneath their lids, but it was so hard to open them again. "Mateo, what are you doing home so early?"

"Something didn't feel right to me ever since you were in the hospital last night so I came straight home to check on you. What's going on? You're sweating like *shit*."

I heard his voice, but it was like I was floating through some made-up universe, and his voice was part of some hidden entity I couldn't find. I was able to open my eyes again seconds later. I focused on the father of the little baby inside of me. "Oh. Hey." I rubbed my eyes, but I was still so...incredibly...sleepy. "Hey. Ummm, I've gotta go to the hospital."

"What? The hospital for what?"

"They think I'm sick. My temp is high." I rubbed my eyes again and tried my best to sit up with my huge belly.

Mateo lovingly felt my forehead with the back of his hand. Though barely awake, I was able to appreciate his tenderness. "Dammit, Megan, you're hot as shit!" I nodded in agreement, unable to find the strength to verbally respond. He then placed the same hand onto my belly, in several different spots, pressing lightly against his son, who was hidden safely underneath my belly's skin. After about a minute, we both felt the baby kick and were reassured.

"How high is the fever?"

I tried to smile through my near-delirium. "It's 104.3, Mateo."

"Uh, yeah, that's too high." He reached out his hand to me. I gratefully took it. "Come on. Let's go."

I suddenly remembered Caleb in my fogginess. "But what about Caleb? He's at Nick's house..."

After a split second of thinking, Mateo told me, "Don't worry. Let me help you into the car and then I'll go talk to his mom. Maybe he can stay until we get back."

It was a struggle, but I kept my smile. "Ok...good. Thank you so much, Mateo."

• • •

The high fever was from Chorioamnionitis, an infection that ended up rupturing my amniotic sac too soon before the baby's actual due date.

"Chorioamnionitis?" I was confused and still amazingly sleepy, the heavy dose of antibiotics not taking effect yet. "How did I get that?"

The doctor turned to me and folded his arms across his chest.

"Well, it's inflammation of the placenta, and typically begins pretty suddenly. What usually happens is the placenta becomes infected with bacteria, which then travels directly to the baby's amniotic sac and causes it to tear prematurely. Most of the time, the mother is completely unaware of this tear. She then starts to drip fluid, *another* thing she's probably unaware of, as well. This can then lead to infection of both the amniotic fluid *and* the baby because the usually protected fluid is now exposed to everything."

I continued to watch the doctor as I took in everything he was saying, my heart not even able to begin her nervous race because she was as tired as the rest of my body. My mind was able to run, though, and I thought about the last huge fight Mateo and I–

"—try not to worry Ms. Harris." I suddenly felt the doctor's gentle touch on my shoulder. "We're going to induce labor as soon as possible, though, to get the baby out of harm's way."

It took every effort I had to swallow the huge lump growing inside my throat.

Dr. Kaparsi took his hand down and looked at me with a warm smile. I was grateful for that. "Don't worry too much, Megan. He'll be tiny, and he'll probably need to stay in the NICU for the next couple of months, but many six-month-ers do well."

I looked up, and didn't know if I believed him or not. But I felt horrible, and knew that if this sickness had taken me down so easily, it must be doing havoc on the innocent one inside me.

Things were progressing too fast, and I was scared.

• • •

"Are you sure that this is what needs to be done?" That was Mateo, who stood protectively by my bedside. "Since they started the antibiotics on her, she seems to be a little more with it now. I mean, her face is still pale as hell, but... "

Dr. Kaparsi gave both of us a reassuring smile. "Yes, this is, in my opinion, what is absolutely necessary, for the health of both the baby *and* Megan." Dr. Kaparsi fixed his attention on me again. "You do understand, Megan—there's no other way? The baby is sick, too. He needs to come out."

I took a look at Mateo, peering into his dark eyes to draw all the strength I could gather from him since he seemed to be in control. His eyes told me that it was going to be okay.

• • •

Mateo was there for me that evening. After Dr. Kaparsi carefully took my legs out of the metal stirrups, Mateo helped me into a wheelchair and followed the doctor down to the delivery room. Through my feverish fogginess, however, my body still managed to express my worry about the impending induction through sweaty palms. Nevertheless, once I got settled into bed and had an epidural placed in anticipation of the treacherous labor pains, I began to settle.

Mateo stayed by my side the whole time that I was in labor. At one point, I had to use the bathroom, but I couldn't leave the bed since the epidural had temporarily immobilized my legs. So Mateo got the pink bedpan from one of the room's shelves, and helped me to get onto it. He even emptied the urine from it when I was finished.

Hours were passing by slowly, and in the interim, Mateo sat in the chair next to me, making phone calls to family and friends, trying to make arrangements for Caleb, and informing everyone that his son was about to be born. He was *so excited*. He even told me, after a short conversation with his mother over the phone, that the woman told him to tell me she loved me—an incredible shock to me, knowing that she thought in the beginning of my and Mateo's relationship that I was just using him to help me raise Caleb. Who would've thought?

He left me only one time, and that was to get something to eat from the hospital's cafeteria, and when he returned, he fell asleep. I watched him as he slept next to me by my bed. He had his fitted hat over his eyes, looking sexy as ever, and I felt...*safe*. God I hoped we could make things work after the baby came.

At 7 p.m. I felt the urge to push. Even though Mateo was excited about the birth of his son, I was terrified. Since I was only six months pregnant, the doctors had told me that the baby would have to stay in the NICU until my actual due date, three months from then. I didn't know what to expect, and I was frightened for this new life that was about to make its entrance into the world, way too early. I buzzed for the nurse, turned to Mateo, and gently woke him.

"Mateo...Mateo..." I whispered his name and tugged a little at his shirt. I waited for him to open his eyes.

"Yeah, what's up?" he whispered.

"I gotta push. Wake up."

I watched him yawn, adjust his hat, then move up inside his chair. I suddenly squinted as another contraction clutched my insides, and the urge to push felt even greater as time ticked along. The nurse who had started my pitocin drip earlier walked into the room at that point, smiled, and asked me what I needed. I lifted my index finger, signaling for her to wait a second until the contraction faded, biting down hard on my bottom lip while the grip on my insides lasted, then told her that I thought it was time for me to push the baby out.

"I feel a lot of pressure, like he's trying to come out," I told nurse Mindy.

I watched her eyes grow with surprise. "Of course!" She briskly walked over towards the contraction monitor and examined the paper that printed the rise and fall of my contractions. "I think you're right. Not a problem; let me get Dr. Kaparsi. Hold on for me, okay?"

By the time Dr. Kaparsi and the NICU team came back into my room and attempted to check my cervix, the baby's head was already crowning. In three pushes, the poor little baby was out, and made his debut into the world with a mere cry that sounded like a little lamb. But I couldn't hold him because he was way too sick and the doctors had to carry him off to the incubator quickly to stabilize his breathing. I was still worried, and Mateo seemed concerned too, as I watched him watch *them* intubate our son. After almost twenty-five minutes had passed, Mindy very carefully placed the baby in front of me just so I could see him, and asked me and Mateo what his name was. I let Mateo answer since it was already given that he would name our son.

"It's Trevon Isaiah." He said it clearly and proudly so that his son would know what his name was...and so that I could hear how he had considered my choice of name after all, even *if* he had made it just a middle name.

13

Nothing There

I watched Mateo quickly disappear behind the off-white front door as he held something small and box-like between his two hands. When the door slammed behind him, the darkness of that morning's events immediately began to fill the empty space. I waited for one whole minute for Mateo to remember me...for him to come back for me...for him to even *lock the damn door behind him* to keep me safe while I was still inside. But he did none of these things.

I suddenly remembered the memory box that the hospital had given us a little over one hour before. My tired eyes moved from the front door to the glass dining table where the box had been left when we returned home from the hospital 20 minutes before. But it wasn't there. I squinted some and searched harder—I even got up and made my way to the table. Sifted carefully through the unopened mail and the pile of paperwork from the baby's short stay at the hospital. Nope, nothing. That's when my mind registered that the small and box-like object that had been in Mateo's hand was the memory box. He had secretly taken it with him when he hauled ass to get out of that apartment...and away from me.

I wiped at my eye, which had begun tearing again, and trudged back to the maroon sofa. I sat down, folded my legs into myself, and picked up the small stuffed dinosaur that had kept Isaiah company for the remainder of his days inside his tiny incubator. I laid my head against the hard armrest and cuddled the toy next to my chest. I listened to the silence. I thought about Mateo and how, in that instance of his leaving me in the apartment alone, I realized that he completely, without a doubt, hated my guts.

At 2:20 that morning, August 10, 2004, Dr. Kaparsi had called to let us know that Isaiah was not doing so well...that even though our baby had received a blood transfusion the night before, it hadn't done much to increase his oxygen levels. I was sleeping when the phone rang, and was having trouble grasping onto what the doctor was telling me. So I asked him if Mateo and I should meet him there at the hospital.

"Well, yes...I think you should. I mean, he may soon start to respond to the oxygen therapy we're giving him, but it may be a good idea to come."

I gently shook Mateo until he awakened. Relayed the news to him just as the doctor had relayed it to me. But he had rubbed my back and told me to pray...that everything was going to be alright. Without wanting to, I obeyed, closing my eyes tightly and *willing* myself to believe that he was right.

When Dr. Keparsi called again at 4:10 a.m. I let Mateo answer the phone hoping that our baby's doctor could finally convince him that we needed to be at the hospital. After getting off the phone, he sat up slowly and looked at me:

"Do you want to go to the hospital?"

I stared at him through the dark of the bedroom, wondering what universe he was currently living in, but not having the courage to ask. I didn't want to upset him, as I was appreciating the very rare calm that we were experiencing since I was ordered to stay out of work to safely prepare for Isaiah's birth. Instead, I told him *yes* and calmly slipped on my clothes through the still of the early morning, knowing deep in my soul that there was no need to rush. When we finally arrived at the hospital at 5:45, Isaiah had already passed.

After the nurses had ushered us gently inside the sterile NICU, I sobbed quietly behind the curtain that separated us from the other babies who were still alive. Surprisingly, Mateo held onto my shoulders as he cried silently while I held onto my baby, hating every fiber inside my body for not having been there to hold my son's tiny hand as he passed from life into death. But I bundled him as close to me as I could and whispered repeatedly how sorry I was, drowning his pretty brown face with tears that would never stop flowing.

· · ·

Morning drifted away into the late afternoon and somewhere in between, I had fallen asleep. At 4:30 p.m., I woke up to the soft buzzing of my cell next to my head. I sleepily lifted my head, grateful for any kind of contact from the outside world. There was a text message from Kelly, letting me know that she had finally woken up from her nap since getting home from her night shift that morning, and that she would be on her way soon. I sent her a response text back, telling her *thank you* and informing her to just let herself in...that the door would be unlocked. I searched through my cell for any other messages or calls that I might have missed from Mateo while I had been sleeping. But there was nothing there.

I closed my phone and pulled my legs over the sofa. I leaned forward and looked at the kitchen table again, wondering where Mateo could be with our memory box. Suddenly, without wanting to, I heard the excited sounds of happy children playing outside, and my heart sank into my belly. I thought about Caleb at that point and how, even though I hated being left alone in the apartment, I was just thankful that he had been able to stay with my mother during this whole ordeal.

I wiped at my eyes once again and ran my hand through my uncombed hair. From the time Mateo and I had gotten back into the car after leaving Isaiah's little body at the hospital, to the time Mateo had put the car in gear and left the hospital's parking garage, I sensed that something immediately changed between us. For a second, while in that NICU, I thought that we were going to be okay after he had tried to console me the minute we saw Isaiah's lifeless body...I had actually thought we were going to be okay. Even though our relationship had been a difficult one for the past *forever*, I was so sure that we were going to be just fine—because he had tried to console me after our baby had passed.

But on our way back home, I noticed the way his jaw seemed to clench every time I cautiously turned to look at him from the passenger seat. He also kept his hardened face straight as he fully concentrated on the traffic ahead of him, indicating to me that somewhere deep inside of him, he wanted to blame me for what just happened, like he did with everything else. I just *felt* it. So on the painfully quiet car ride back to Temple Hills, I knew, without his even saying it, that he was quickly searching for a way to blame me for Isaiah's death.

And when he swiftly unlocked our front door and headed straight to the narrow hallway bathroom with his shoes still on his feet—without even making sure that I had made it in before the slam of the door—and walked right back outside without so much as telling me to *fuck off,* his hatred for me was confirmed.

I looked down at my closed hands, which rested on top of my lap; opened them...clasped them back together again, then reopened them. I reached for Isaiah's dinosaur and held its softness to my nose. I breathed in the subtle newborn scent left behind by him and leaned over into my thighs, letting out my cries into the palms of my hands.

• • •

By 6:10 p.m., I had managed to move from the sofa in order to switch the floor lamp to its dim setting and finally use the bathroom after more than 12 hours. When I was done, I decided to take a seat at our dining room table. Actually, it wasn't *our* dining room table; it was just *Mateo's*. And in the time that I was left alone to mourn the loss of our baby by myself, I had quickly begun to feel as if I were no longer welcomed inside the home that I had initially moved into almost a year ago. As if, with the death of our baby came with it the death of my and Mateo's relationship, and any other attachment that I previously had to him.

As I sat next to the empty space that the missing memory box had left, I opened my cell once more, just in case I had missed any calls from Mateo—or anyone else—while I had been in the bathroom a few moments before. Nothing. Just then, I heard the slight turn of the door handle, and I was hopeful that it could be him.

"Hey sweetie." Kelly quietly announced her arrival as she carefully stepped inside the living room, bending over to take off her sandals, which she left next to the neat collection of shoes by the entrance. She then slowly and quietly closed and locked the off-white door and stared at me for a minute, her eyes teary with compassion and understanding.

I mustered a quiet *Hey,* momentarily disappointed that Kelly wasn't Mateo, but glad that she was finally there with me. I watched her as she walked over towards the glass table, holding a large plastic bag in her left hand. She set it down opposite from where I sat, and immediately, the smell of baked chicken invaded my nasal passages.

"Well, I brought you guys some food from Boston Market. I know it's not much, but hopefully it will help a little." Kelly pulled out a vanilla-colored chair and sat down. "Where *is* Mateo, by the way? I didn't see the car outside..."

I sniffled and wiped at my nose, keeping my focus on the bag from Boston Market. "I don't know. As soon as we made it back from the hospital, he left—"

"—he *left*?"

I nodded my head and made eye contact with Kelly, who now looked puzzled as her green eyes began to search my own for an explanation. "Yep, he left."

She kept her eyes on me for a second and breathed in slowly and deeply. "And Caleb's with your mother?"

I breathed in, as well, trying hard to fight the tears that were finding their way back to the edges of my eyelids as I thought about my five-year-old and whether or not my mother had told him that his brother had passed. "Yes," I simply responded. Veronica had gotten Caleb from Mateo once Mateo had returned to the apartment after I'd given birth.

I watched Kelly as she continued to search my eyes for some inkling as to what I needed for her to do in that instant. But I crossed my arms over one another and hugged myself tight, choosing to look away from her and so I could refocus my attention on that Boston Market bag, trying with all my might to block out the youthful voices that continued to float into the apartment, uninvited, from the outside. I hugged myself even tighter, feeling a sudden chill in the air, even though it must've been at least 85 degrees outside.

"He has the memory box," I suddenly heard myself blurt out

after a while.

"I'm sorry, he has the *what*?"

I lifted my heavy eyes and fixed them back onto Kelly's. "The baby's memory box," I simply stated. "I would show you pictures of the baby and everything—even a lock of his hair they had clipped for us—but Mateo took the fucking box. Took the fucking box and left me by my *fucking self*, Kelly." I was angry, hopeless, ashamed of myself, and regretting the day I met Mateo, all at once. As memories of holding my poor sweet baby rushed into my mind, I had no choice but to give way to the uncontrollable tremors that began taking over my body until I was forced to openly sob in front of my friend.

Kelly hurried over to my side of the table, knelt down in front of me, and wrapped her arms securely around my waist. I held onto her as tight as I could and cried my sorrow into her shoulder. The nonstop tears that had been a part of that whole miserable day surfaced from a place buried deep inside of me that I had never known existed before that morning. I wanted to escape *outside* myself—be anywhere and be anybody other than where I was and *who* I was at that moment—and get away from that horrible darkness that now hovered closely over me...that refused to say when, or *if*, it would ever leave my world.

Kelly let me go and rested her hands on top of my knee caps. She looked up at me through reddened eyes, and I was grateful that *somebody* was there, feeling my pain with me. "You're going to be okay. Now, I can't tell you *when* exactly, but know that one day, this will come to pass. Okay?"

I looked into her eyes and whispered *Okay*.

• • •

By the time evening gave way to early night, I was bathed, clothed in fresh pajamas, and my hair was combed into two long French braids, courtesy of Kelly. As we sat side-by-side on the maroon sofa, I flipped open my cell phone for the fourth time that day to see if I had missed any calls/texts from Mateo—or anyone else—but there was nothing there. I sighed and let my head fall against the back of the sofa.

"Hey...let's turn the TV on," Kelly suggested, patting my knee gently. "I don't like the thought of this house being so quiet right now." I kept my head back and my eyes towards the ceiling as I felt Kelly lift her body from the sofa. Two seconds later, Alex Trebek's voice filled the lonely living room with his announcement of *Final Jeopardy*.

I took my eyes from the ceiling and rested my head onto Kelly's slender shoulder once she sat back down. I breathed in the floral scent that emanated from her curly blonde hair, and closed my eyes as I inhaled her peace, finding myself desperately wanting the same.

• • •

At 9 p.m., Kelly gently informed me that she had to head home and get ready for another night shift at the hospital. I got up from the sofa and walked with my friend to the front door and thanked her again for coming to my aid. She kissed my cheek and wrapped her arms around me. I inhaled the fragrance of the flowers from her hair once more as I leaned my heavy burden against her small, but strong frame. God, I didn't want her to leave.

When she let me go, she took my hand and squeezed it lovingly. "Drink the tea I made for you earlier and take the Benadryl so you can sleep...and I'll call you in the morning."

I nodded my head obediently, swallowing my urge to cry again as I watched Kelly leave the apartment. After I closed the door behind her, the darkness that had stayed at bay during Kelly's stay quickly began to move in on me once again. I stood by the front door for a whole minute, unsure of what to do next. Finally, I made my way back to the sofa, collected the small dinosaur that had been sitting by his lonesome, and sat down, bringing my legs up close to my chin. Before covering myself with my oversized cotton robe, I reached for my cell that had been resting on the sofa's arm, and checked for any missed calls or messages that I might have missed from Mateo while I had been saying goodbye to Kelly. But there was nothing there.

14

Prey

"Let me talk to you for a second."

I dropped what I was doing, catching my breath abruptly inside my throat. His usual deep and soothing voice had become foreign to me since the death of Isaiah, and the sudden sound of it frightened my insides. Suddenly, I realized how cold and quiet the bedroom was, even in the hot month of August. The only thing I could hear was the muffled sounds of the PlayStation, which Mateo's cousin Travis was playing in the living room some fifty feet away. Considering he had at least four young children, spread between just as many mothers, I didn't understand why he had nothing better to do on a Saturday evening. But there he was, in our apartment, playing a fucking video game.

Mateo didn't speak, so I slowly resumed my breathing. With my back still facing him, I placed the socks in the top drawer of the oak dresser where they belonged, and gently closed the drawer. I then cautiously turned my attention to him and waited—arms by my sides, heart thudding inside my ears—for him to speak.

"You killed my son. You were the reason why he died."

My jaw fell. Mateo's words seemed to have leapt from his mouth and raced towards me with a punch that delivered more power than his own fists could ever achieve. All I could do was stare dumbly at him. Stared at him as he continued to watch me through his narrowed eyes, as if he were a voracious lion...and I was his targeted prey.

After a moment in the silence of that room, I closed my mouth and swallowed, completely thrown off by his vicious accusation. His dark eyes began to scare me, and after swiping my tongue across my dry lips, I told him quietly (and respectfully):

Well...since you feel that way...I'm just gonna pack my bags and leave.

Even though his words stunned me, I think I'd been waiting for a reason to vacate the apartment he and I had shared for the past year. Since Isaiah died three weeks ago, our living arrangements had become unbearable: Mateo barely had anything to say to me since leaving our lifeless baby at the hospital, choosing to avoid me at all costs. His presence at the apartment was also becoming a thing of the past, as he now spent most of his time with Travis. My five-year-old son Caleb was having trouble processing what exactly was going on, and Mateo's sudden decision to ignore his presence made me realize that he now hated *my son* for still being alive when *his son* didn't make it past his six days here on Earth.

My movements robotic, I turned to exit our small bedroom with the intention of grabbing my suitcases from the hallway closet as fast as I could. Reaching for the door knob, I made a step to leave, but Mateo beat me to it, instantly jumping from his place on the floor and charging towards me like a determined football player. In one swift motion, he effortlessly turned me around so I was facing him, grabbed me by my neck, and lifted me inches from the floor before slamming my back against the small space that separated the dresser from the bedroom door. His long black hand began to squeeze *hard*, instantly stopping the flow of oxygen between my throat and my nose as he pinned me to the wall. I felt my eyes being forced from their sockets as I watched his own eyes morph into something I had never seen before in my twenty-four years.

"*You're gonna fucking listen to what I have to say,*" Mateo spat at me, his once-handsome features turning demonic by the seconds that seemed to take forever to pass. And that's when I knew this was it. That *this* was the moment that all the days of silence and avoidance were going to prove to be nothing but a simmering pot of anger, blame, and utter devastation that finally reached its boiling point, at *this very moment.*

"You're gonna *fucking listen to me* because you haven't given a *SHIT* about my feelings since my son died!"

He released me. I collapsed on the floor, gasping for any breath I could find, feeling a wetness begin to make a path from my nose to my mouth. I carefully touched the liquid with my fingers and saw that it was blood. I didn't dare look directly at Mateo, though, as my peripheral noticed him calmly reclaiming his place by the closet.

"Look at me, Megan. *LOOK* at *me!*"

I started to cry, not wanting to oblige his request and give away any remaining power and self-respect I still had left. After strangling me with a rage he had never used on me before, he was now demanding that I obey him, like I was his fucking child. I was confused. He had *never* choked me before. *Never* held my life in the palm of his bare hands like he had just done. And what usually preceded our fights was my yelling and screaming about something I felt he had done wrong. But I had been quiet this time. I hadn't yelled. I hadn't screamed. I hadn't been in his face, complaining about something or the other. I had even offered to leave. And normally, after our fights ended, a switch would automatically flip inside his brain, compelling him to feel terribly about what just transpired, and he'd begin to wipe my tears away...

"*LOOK AT ME!*"

My head snapped to attention and I reluctantly faced my dead son's father. Just then, I heard a man curse from the living room and remembered that Travis was in the apartment. I *knew* he could hear what was going on—why didn't he come in to help me?

"Now you're going to listen to what I have to say, and you're gonna watch me cry..."

Oh, my God. What the fuck is wrong with him?

"...and you're *not* gonna leave until I'm finished. *You hear me?*"

I nodded, and at that point, a mixture of hatred and agony summoned from the deepest and most secret depths of Mateo's soul quickly appeared in the form of dark tears, replacing the comical eyes I had once known only weeks before, when I was still carrying our child. I cried even harder as I listened to him tell me how it was my fault that Isaiah died...that he had told me that I didn't have to continue to work my physically-demanding job while I was pregnant...that after our baby died, I had never once asked him how he was doing. How could I? He was *never* home anymore. And as he talked and vented and used me for his verbal punching bag, I cried even harder. I cried because my throat hurt. I cried for my dead baby who had shitty parents who could only leave his body behind in a cold hospital because they couldn't afford a proper funeral. And I cried because I sat there and let a man continue to abuse me, even in the wake of losing a child.

Before I knew it, he had me in his arms, crying his heart out into my chest, telling me over and over again that he didn't mean to say those things, that he had a problem, and that he was sorry he hurt me, *once again*. He then laid me down onto my back and began to undress me from the waist down, telling me over and over again that we could try again...that we could make another baby.

I let him have sex with me, bleeding and everything from giving birth less than a month ago. My soul faded away with each thrust he forced, becoming as nonexistent as Isaiah's had when his little body finally tired of the disease that claimed him from the moment he was born.

• • •

When I woke up the next morning, my debit card was missing. My neck sore and my body still trembling from Mateo's wrath, I quietly showered and dressed before going for my debit card so that I could withdraw my share of the money to renew the lease for the next 12 months. When I couldn't find the Bank of America card that I religiously kept inside my wallet, I began to panic.

"Mateo, I can't find my debit card anywhere—have you seen it?"

He could barely look at me. I wasn't sure if guilt and shame from the night before took over his eyes, or if he merely couldn't stand the sight of me if he was still blaming me for Isaiah's death. He shook his head slowly. "No, I haven't seen it. You look everywhere?"

I blew out my panic, my heart slowly starting to pick up its pace. It just so happened that Mateo almost choked the life out of me the evening before, my debit card was now missing, and...it just so happened...that Travis was nowhere to be found. I didn't know if he had spent the night or left while Mateo had me trapped in our bedroom. But I had always kept my handbag on the door handle of the coat closet, which was inches from the front door. I called my bank and reported the card missing.

I was outraged to learn that $600 had been withdrawn from the ATM, located less than a mile from the apartment. And it was taken out in three separate transactions of $200 each just a couple of hours ago. I looked at Mateo, who seemed to be waiting patiently to hear what the bank had to say. It wasn't unusual for me to hand over my debit card to him, in case he needed to buy some things for Caleb while I was at work, so he knew my PIN. There was no way he could have given the PIN to Travis...?

"Do you want us to do an investigation?" the customer service agent was asking me on the other end of the line.

I took my eyes off Mateo, tears beginning to form for the thousandth time since Isaiah had passed. I couldn't believe this was happening to me...not now...not at this time...not when I *just* lost my baby. "Yes, *please*," I almost begged her. "And can you tell me again what time these transactions took place?"

"Surely, Ms. Harris. The first withdrawal was at 7:45 this morning, the other one was at 7:47, and the last one was at 7:49. If you go to the police station and press formal charges, we'll be able to bring up the picture of the person who did this, since our ATMs have built-in cameras..."

I pulled the cell phone from my ear and looked at the time on the front of the phone's screen. It was now nearing 10 a.m. At 7:45, I was still asleep, tucked away in the bedroom with Mateo. I *knew* I had my debit card on me yesterday, because I had used it to pay my cell phone bill.

"Okay...yes, I'll go to the police station as soon as I can to file an official report."

"Okay, Ms. Harris. And in the meantime, we'll do an investigation on this end and have the money back into your account within seven to ten business days."

I told her *thank you* and ended the call.

I wiped the water from my eyes and threw my cell into my bag, making a mental note to keep it on me at all times from now on, even if I had to sleep with the damn thing around my shoulder.

"What did they say, Megan?"

I didn't answer Mateo. When he saw I wasn't budging, he came over to the dining room table where I sat and looked at me.

"Your cousin stole my money."

His face drew a blank, and then suddenly turned into an expression of understanding. Was this planned? Did he put his cousin up to stealing my money? Or was he not at all surprised that Travis would do such a *bastard* thing?

I took a hard look at Mateo for the first time since we got back from the hospital the day Isiaiah had died. He had lost weight—maybe ten pounds—his hair was growing uncontrollably curly, defying his usual close cut, and he still wore the bracelet the hospital had given him weeks ago, identifying him as Isaiah's father so he could get into the NICU with no problems. He was unrecognizable.

"I'm gonna call my aunt and see what we can do."

I didn't want him to call his aunt for help. She had been nice enough to me during the couple of interactions I had with her, but I knew she didn't like me. I said nothing, though, a newfound fear of him now buried inside of me after last night. All I could do was remain at the table, limp as a Raggedy Ann doll, and watch him disappear into our bedroom with the cordless phone in his hand.

Twenty minutes later, he emerged and took a seat back at the dining room table. His thick, once kissable lips began to turn upright at the corners of his mouth, and for a second, I was grateful because I hadn't seen him smile in weeks. But as I continued to watch his face, his mouth began to twist into something sinister and self-satisfying.

"Aunt Alicia said that we should each go to our banks and apply for a loan, and that maybe you should go apply for one first. She also said that if you can't get your life right with God, then we can't be together."

My heart tripped over a couple of beats before slamming against my chest for a short pause. *I'm sorry—what??* I stared at him, completely dumbfounded, as his smile dissolved into complete smugness. My mouth ran dry, and before I knew what I was doing, I stood, absentmindedly knocking over the chair that I had been sitting in. Tears began to blind my eyes once more.

I began yelling. "*I'm* the one who's supposed to go ask for a loan?!? It was *your cousin* who stole *my money*! And then, you ask *the same aunt* for advice...*the same aunt* who had *NOTHING* to do with me when my baby died? *Fuck, Mateo*—it was *her son* who stole MY MONEY!"

He just watched me—his face void of any emotion except pure joy from the nervous breakdown I was having in front of him. Aunt Alicia had been able to convince him that I was the enemy all along—from the very day we lost Isaiah, when she had provided comfort for him at her family's house while I was left alone in the apartment to grieve by myself. I was quickly losing it because not only did Mateo hate me, his *family* hated me, too. And that meant I had no one left on my side. *Fuck! What could she possibly say to him to make him believe that it was my fault our child died??!!* I was in a world that didn't belong to me anymore, and things were spinning out of control faster than I could handle. I started to hyperventilate, my chest rising and falling uncontrollably. Why couldn't this nightmare *just end?!* I opened my handbag—the same one Mateo's cousin had helped himself to just hours before—and began rifling through its contents until I found my prescription bottle. Just then, I heard a loud, sarcastic smirk from across the table before I heard Mateo announce:

See, look at the pills you're taking—SHIT! You're not even fit to be in any kind of relationship with me! Look at you—you're pathetic.

No wonder our son died!

Loud bellows of laughter then erupted from my son's father as I quickly forced the cap off the medicine bottle and popped two Ativans into my mouth, swallowing them down with only traces of spit.

I put my prescription bottle back into my bag and, in a brave move, told him:

I'm leaving. I can't take this anymore. I can't take this anymore, Mateo!

And then he slowly and dramatically held his black hands out in fake resignation and asked me:

Do you need me to help you pack?

And that's when the dams gave way, and the tears started spilling over the bottom lids of my eyes. I cried openly and desperately. "*WHAT?* You really want me *to leave??*"

"If you're not gonna get your life right with God, we can't work this out, Megan. C'mon—" he casually shrugged a shoulder—"I'll help you pack."

I couldn't believe what was happening. I walked around to the other side of the table where Mateo stood, clutching the glass table with my hand, as if it were the only thing keeping me from falling over. Huge tears continued to splash sloppily everywhere. "Mateo, *please*! I don't want to go. I just need you to listen to me. Talk to *me*, not *your aunt*. I need you to *JUST LISTEN TO ME!*" My whole body shook, but I continued to watch Mateo as I waited for some kind of miracle to happen. Waited for him to change the carefree look on his face, and to reach out and hold me, and to tell me that he was sorry, like he always did whenever things went too far.

But instead, he lifted his hand, cracked his mouth open, and waved *good-bye.*

I stared, wide-eyed, crazed, still holding onto the glass dinner table for dear life.

"Bye, *MEGAN,*" he sarcastically reiterated.

My mouth dropped, the tears refusing to stop. I wiped my face and forced my mouth to close. I looked directly into Mateo's eyes and searched hard for the man I thought I knew. "Mateo, *nooo.*" I spoke softly through my tears. "I'm sorry." I abhorred the weak girl who stood there, begging a man she *knew* didn't deserve her. But as I watched her during the temporary out-of-body experience I was having, I understood that was all she *could do*, because at that very point, she had no other choice.

He placed his hands gently on both of my thin shoulders, jerking me back to my reality as he turned me towards the hall that led to our bedroom. He then removed his left hand and used it to point straight down the narrow hall towards the room, repeating his disgust for me, in case I hadn't caught it moments ago:

Bye Megan. Get your things and go.

"All That Matters"

All that matters is you–
Not the vengeful punishment taken for the baby's death,
There is nothing left to do.

The hits, the slaps, the kisses that came so few–
But in a severely fractured soul,
All that matters is you.

Even after the heavy-handed hatred you spew–
The fresh raindrops that now mix with old tears
Wipe away any pain that you continue to do.

And the handsome eyes that watch from above–
That totally belie the disgust you've felt since the day of our son's
    demise–
All that matters is you.

Self is lost, but the body's not through–
No matter how much you destroy,
"Love" is gonna continue, no matter what you do…

…because at this very moment…where time and space stand still,
so the world can revolve around yours again–
Because all that really matters will always, only, be you,
No matter what you say, no matter what you do.

15

All That Matters

Words mean nothing, and actions mean everything.

I was broken after the death of my newborn son. And staying away from the person who had abruptly cut me off less than a month after the sickness devoured Isaiah's tiny body was impossible. Two months after we lost Isaiah, I begged Mateo to take me back into his life. Begged him like an addict begs for her next hit. Because inside my severely shattered mind, I was able to make myself believe that Mateo really did love me and that since we lost our baby, that *must* be the reason he had treated me worse than an animal.

But he treated you like an animal even BEFORE you gave birth to Isaiah. For all we know, that's probably the reason why you went into labor so...

"Stop it!" I hissed towards my conscience, instantly putting my hands up to cover both my ears. I squeezed my eyes shut, and when I reopened them, I took my hands down slowly, sneaking looks from my left to my right to make sure there was no one else present on the landing of Mateo's apartment. I then looked down into my hand and gently unfolded the white piece of paper I used to write Mateo's note an hour before I gathered the courage (stupidity) to go back to the place I was told never to go back to :

Mateo,

I love you...and I'm so sorry we lost Isaiah. But I still love you and I need you. Please don't keep me shut out. Here is my beeper number: (301) 702-1002.

Megan

I had a cell phone, but the service had been suspended since I was barely making ends meet after Mateo threw me out. But I was able to get a beeper, which only cost $25/month, something I was able to manage as I got back on my feet.

I folded the paper back and carefully slid it through the crack that separated the off-white door from the building's frame, afterwards peeping through the space to make sure the note fell securely inside Mateo's apartment.

I opened my bag and fished out my newly prescribed bottle of *Celexa* and downed my daily meds with a swallow of bottled water.

• • •

"So did you finally get the keys?"

I smiled back at Kelly and dangled a bronze apartment key in her line of sight, feeling sudden deja vu as I remembered *this same moment* almost a year ago when I had moved away from Mateo *the first time.* "Yep! I've got the keys. The apartment is all mine!"

Kelly jumped up from her sofa and ran to me, giving me a comforting squeeze. "Yay! I knew you would, girl! Now, tell me all about it."

I hunched my shoulders as I followed her back to her comfy beige sofa. There wasn't much to tell. It was an efficiency, just one big room that included the bathroom, the walk-in closet and the ugly kitchen. The apartment was barely big enough to hold a

154

daybed inside of it. But I had a place to call my own, once again, that was also (conveniently) close to the father of my dead child. And just in case he decided to ring my beeper after getting my message...

I hunched my shoulders again, and turned my face away from Kelly as the excitement of possibly seeing Mateo again began to warm my interior. But I couldn't let Kelly in on it; it would remain my secret. I shook my head and refocused my attention on my friend. Kelly had given me and Caleb a temporary place of solace, once again, after Isaiah died. And I was doing really well for someone who had to fight each day to keep from completely drowning in her own sorrow: I still had my job at the hospital, still had my car, and I was able to find my new place only two months after Mateo had told me to leave.

"It's small—"

"—nothing wrong with that!"

"And it's just an efficiency—"

"—again, nothing wrong with that."

I nodded my head. "Yep, especially since I won't even have Caleb anymore."

Kelly's green eyes glistened as they held my own brown ones in place. "But you know what, Moogie (the sweet nickname she had come up with when we first met)? He'll be *just fine* with your mom. Plus, you need the time to yourself to pull yourself back together."

I watched her eyes and continued to breathe evenly and deeply, as I felt my heart start to pick up her anxious pace once more. "Thanks." I gently squeezed her hand. "I've gotta go make sure Caleb is packed and ready to go soon."

• • •

I met my mother at her house an hour later. Caleb was showered, dressed in a pair of khaki shorts and a red polo shirt, with a child-sized suitcase by his side that was packed neatly with clothes and his favorite stuffed teddy bear. I felt incredibly stupid as I waited outside my mother's oak door, knowing that she would relish the moment that I handed my son over to her for an indefinite period of time. Having him all to herself proved everything she'd been claiming for the five years of Caleb's life—that I was a sub-par mother who had no business being responsible for anyone's child.

My heart jerked when I finally heard the door creak open, and immediately, my mother's French perfume filled my nose with a scent that I'd grown to hate. However, our eyes never met as she immediately looked down at her grandson and greeted him warmly. How she could love Caleb so much when she hated his mother just as equally was beyond my cognitive ability to understand.

Caleb's innocent eyes lit at his grandmother's smile, and though I hated having to do what I was doing, I was grateful that at least Caleb was all for going with his grandmother. I bent down to meet his height and looked into his eyes.

"Mommy's going to leave you for a little bit so that you can start kindergarten. But I'll see you this weekend, okay?"

Caleb gave a hearty nod, clutching his gray and white teddy bear a little tighter against his small chest. "Okay, Mommy. I'll be okay."

I stood up and forced myself to meet the icy and satisfied glaze of my mother, as we both tried our best to look away from one another, while still looking *at* one another. How I wished she could've been a little more supportive, or just plain...*human*. But I had to keep reminding myself that this arrangement was for the best and that it was a blessing she was able to do it. Since I didn't have a place yet to call home, I couldn't register Caleb for his first year of school, as the Maryland/D.C./Virginia area required a permanent place of residence to enroll a child. It was now the end of September; school had already started way back in August, and I wouldn't be able to sign my new lease until the middle of the next month. I didn't want to continue holding Caleb back while I struggled to get my shit together.

• • •

"I didn't mean to do what I did, Megan. But I just couldn't take what happened to our son. I just couldn't take that shit..."

I paused at the stop sign on the corner of Autumn Drive and Fitch Avenue, checking for passing cars. I let the car stall for a moment as I looked over at Mateo, the father of my deceased infant. He had gotten the letter I left for him inside his apartment and beeped me his number a week after I took Caleb to his grandmother's. When I suddenly heard the three quick, high-pitched "beeps" sound off in the middle of the night, I was elated when I saw Mateo's phone number light the tiny screen. The depression I'd been feeling since Isaiah's death and my having to leave Caleb with my mother suddenly lifted with just the sound of Mateo's voice, and now I had something to finally look forward to.

"It's okay," I replied softly. I turned back to the road and proceeded through the intersecting streets at a speed of 15 mph. Mateo and I were perusing the streets that neighbored Mateo's apartment building. With no destination in mind, I carefully drove through the quiet, house-lined streets as I admired the subtle change from summer to early fall, grateful that Mateo and I were no longer fighting. We were finally talking about Isaiah's death, and even though my heart was weighed down with grief, Mateo and I were back to being in the same space together, and that was all that mattered.

"Pull over on the next street," Mateo suddenly said softly, nodding towards his right. I did as I was told and made a gentle right onto a street with four houses and a dead end that opened out to a very wooded area. I parallel-parked the car along with the few other cars that lined the street's sidewalk.

Mateo took off his seatbelt. "C'mon, let's take a walk."

I was confused because I felt like we were trespassing, but I followed suit, unbuckling my seatbelt and getting out of the car. I waited for Mateo to exit before closing my door, and, as if reading my mind, he cracked a small smile and told me:

Don't worry—there's no one out here, Megan. Just trust me.

I watched him close his side and head towards the trunk of my car. He then asked mischievously:

You got a blanket in here?

I smirked. "Yeah, I've got everything in my car since–." I suddenly stopped myself, not wanting to rehash the events from weeks ago. I cleared my throat. "Yeah, I've got a blanket in here"

I used my key to open the trunk of my little white Nissan. When Mateo peered inside, his thick eyebrows rose in surprise at the huge suitcase, medium-sized cardboard box of toiletries, and the two fleece blankets that had taken up residency in my car since he had evicted me from his apartment. He said nothing; instead, he reached for the pink fleece and closed the trunk. With a slight nod of his head, he told me *Come on* and crossed the quiet street to get to the densely wooded area that faced the parallel row of cars. I didn't know what he was up to, but I followed him, as I always did.

We carefully crossed over thorns and long, tangly plants as tiny branches echoed loudly under our shoes. I held both hands out as I balanced myself over the uneven terrain, heart beginning to pound as I wondered if we'd get caught, or if my car would be okay parked in someone else's neighborhood. Thirty feet into the brush, Mateo stopped at a small clearing and laid the fleece blanket on the ground.

"Go ahead. Lie down."

I continued standing, briefly wondering how he knew about this place. Reading my mind again, he looked over at me with the dark eyes I had fallen in love with almost two years before and said:

What's wrong? Sit down. You know I've lived in these parts forever. I've known about this spot since I was a boy.

I raised an eyebrow, suspicious. But he held out his hand and my heart became his again. Such a simple gesture, yet, for me, it carried so much promise—something I desperately needed since the day Isaiah passed.

I gave Mateo my hand and let him lead me to the blanketed ground. The bright reds, yellows, and oranges of fall fell down around us as the trees towered above, blocking out any remaining sunlight. Mateo seductively removed my sandals before removing my panties, and I let him enter me. It didn't matter that we just lost our baby almost two months before, it didn't matter that Mateo had subsequently kicked me out of the apartment he and I had shared, and it didn't matter that I had to end up giving custody of Caleb to Veronica because I now had no legal residence. All that mattered was that particular pause in time when everything around me stood still and I was with the love of my life. And if I could experience this pleasure with him again, after all the misfortune we had suffered together, then I knew I would have a second chance and make this right because he was there with *me*.

My conscience leered at me, and an image of dropping Caleb off with my mother for an uncertain amount of time passed through my head. But I pushed both aside and chose to focus on the now-grayish sky as fresh rain drops began to mix with the tears that began filling my eyes.

• • •

"Megan...?"

I opened my eyes and looked into the eyes of the man that I wanted to be connected to forever, four months after our romp in the forest. And he wanted another baby with me...because he just said it, right? Who was I kidding, though? I was a broken girl. I couldn't stay away from Mateo. He was my life source, and he knew it. We were terrible for one another, but I needed him to complete me—to provide comfort and affirmation so that I never felt alone. And he needed *me*—to provide a place of freedom to live away from his father (since he ended up losing his apartment, even *after* Travis drained my account), as well as transportation to and from work, and a warm body to lie down with whenever he felt the desire. I knew all this—*knew* deep down that Mateo was using me. But as long as he needed me, I still believed I had a chance to make him love me one day.

"You mean that?"

I saw him nod his head slightly through the dark of that small living room while he kept his dark eyes locked onto mine. "Yeah, Megan. I'm serious. For making up for what happened to Isaiah..."

Isaiah. It was the first time I heard my baby son's name come out of Mateo's mouth since he had passed away in August. I nodded my head and whispered *Okay*, slowly releasing the grip I had on Mateo's body so he could resume his rhythm. I was surprised, but overjoyed. And even though his relationship with Caleb was borderline imaginary, his decision to have another baby with me proved that everything was finally going to be okay.

• • •

By the beginning of May, I was showing another rounded belly, less than a year after I gave birth to Isaiah. And even though I never gave my body the time it needed to heal from the last pregnancy, and I was still taking antidepressants for the loss of Isaiah, nothing made me prouder than to head off to my mid-morning classes at the local community college, carrying Mateo's tiny, little baby inside of me again (that was, of course, *after* driving the 50 miles to Ashburn, Virginia to drop him off at his construction job, then turning the car right back around to get to school by 10 a.m.).

I was fucking *delusional.*

I *knew* I was wrong for letting Mateo back into my life, especially back into my *home,* after he'd thrown me out of *his own home* only six months prior. I was also wrong for getting him back and forth to work...for putting so much effort into another man when I couldn't even do it for Caleb. I wanted to believe I was still a good mom because I still had my job, I was now in school, and I was picking Caleb up twice a week to play at my tiny hole-in-the wall apartment with a "step-father" who acted like he could care less. But honestly, I was no kind of mother because no matter what Mateo did to me, my life continued to revolve around his, as if Caleb and I didn't even matter.

• • •

But again, a baby is not a magic potion, old habits die hard, and a new pregnancy wasn't going to suddenly change who Mateo really was. It was now nearing 5 p.m. on a Tuesday evening, and I hadn't seen him since he left for work the day before. When I finally heard his keys jingling inside the door knob, I calmly stood from my place on the daybed, crossed my arms over my growing belly, and got ready.

"Where've you been?"

He gently closed the door, pocketed his set of keys, and looked at me. "What do you mean? I've been at work all day—"

"—you've been at work all day?" That's not what I was asking, and he *knew* it wasn't what I was asking. "I *know* you've been at work all day, Mateo. But why the hell did you stay out *all night*, and with *my car*?"

He gave me an angry smirk before heading off to the little bathroom inside the walk-in closet. "*Your* car?" Megan, you can have *your car* back for all I give a shit." With that, he pulled the extra car key I had given him from his key chain and tossed it at me. "Take your key back. I need to take a shower. I'm not going through this shit with you right now." With that, he turned towards the walk-in closet, making his way into the miniature bathroom.

I let the black key land on the thin carpet. I was in disbelief, as his throwing his key at me was like a slap to my face that yelled, *I don't need your car OR YOU anymore.* And deep down I knew that if he felt he no longer needed me, he could leave at any time, and I just *could not take that.*

I followed him, chest beginning to rise and fall with anger and desperation. "That's *not* fair, Mateo," I yelled at his backside. "That's *not* fair! You can't just take the car and leave the whole night and not even tell me where the hell you've been!"

He stopped. With his lean back still facing me he warned, "Megan, stay the *fuck* away from me."

"Fuck you, Mateo!" I snapped. "You can't just leave like that, with my car, and not even let me know what the fuck you're doing! I'm fucking four months pregnant—you can't keep doing *shit* like this to me!" I should've walked away...let bygones be bygones when he tossed the key at me minutes before. I should've taken the quiet times Mateo left me with to study for my finals, finish school, do something better with my life so that I could provide for Caleb better than what I was doing at the time, like I *knew* I could. Instead, I was arguing back and forth about common decency...with a man who could care *less* about what that was. I knew all of this, and *still*,

162

a year and a dead baby later, could not bring myself to do what I knew was the right thing to do. God, I was pathetic.

He turned and bent down, making sure his dark eyes met mine. "Fuck you, too! I'm a grown-ass man—*don't* tell me what the fuck I can and can't do!"

"I take you to and from work almost every day, Mateo! Every fucking day! You don't pay my car note, you don't pay for the insurance...at best, you may put gas in the damn thing, but that's *all you do*!" Breathless, I paused for a heartbeat as my growing belly moved up and down as I worked to control my erratic breathing. "Where in the fuck *were you* all night, anyway?"

Mateo leaned in closer so that his thick nose was touching mine and his black eyes were making contact with my soul. "*None. Of. Your. Fucking. Business.*" Losing my control, I took a step back and thrust my index finger in his face and screamed:

Stay the fuck away from my car, then!

He balled up his fist and aimed it at my head. But I was able to duck out of range in time as I watched in horror as his closed hand landed inside the cheap drywall behind me. After pulling it out of the huge hole he just made, he took a moment to study his knuckles before setting his furious eyes back onto mine.

"You need to worry less about *me* and more about *getting your son back* from your bitch-ass mother, *Megan!*"

I gasped. Fuck him! Looking him square in the eye, I gathered all the rage and frustration I had felt for the past two years and spat:

"*Fuck you*, Mateo. That's why your sister died!"

I regretted it as soon as the words flew from my mouth, but felt even more remorseful when he grabbed me by my throat and forced my back against the damaged wall. "*Never* say shit about my sister again." He released my neck and I slumped to the floor while holding my belly. Through hot, blinding tears, I watched him, helplessly, as he angrily gathered some of his personal belongings.

I began to cry (that's all I did nowadays). Mateo's sister had been a few years older than him when she died of an aneurysm about ten years ago. I didn't want to say that shit to him, but I wanted him to hurt as badly as I hurt. I wanted him to feel every ounce of pain he made me feel since I had gotten pregnant *the first time,* so I did the only thing I could do, and that was to say the worst thing I could think of that would lacerate his heart. I hated him, and even worse, I hated myself, because instead of just walking away, I stayed and entertained the bullshit.

With my head buried inside my knees, I could barely hear Mateo's rushed movements above my sobs. About two minutes later, however, I heard the front door open and slam shut, and after 30 seconds of nothing but the sound of my heart inside my ears, I knew it was safe to pull my head out of its hiding place. Mateo was now gone, and the only things left were the Ikea daybed, a floor lamp, a small, flat screen TV, my pile of school books, and the unsettling quiet staring right back at me.

16

Junior

I was 23 weeks, 6 days pregnant when my water gave way unexpectedly at the Family Dollar, splashing a clear, quiet mess of amniotic fluid all over my blue sandals. After I was rushed to the hospital, Dr. Daniel was stuck in between doing an emergency C-section and waiting another day to deliver the baby. If the baby could just wait another 10 hours inside of me, until I made it to exactly *24 weeks*, he would have a slightly better chance of surviving.

"Do you know what you want to do?"

I shook my head in confusion, as my heart beat furiously against my ribcage. I knew time was against me and the baby, but I was scared shitless to make the wrong choice.

Dr. Daniel saw the obvious battle going on inside my head and thankfully, I didn't have to give him an answer. He stopped moving the transducer, taking his eyes from the ultrasound image. "Tell you what...what's your boyfriend's name?"

"Mateo."

"And what's his number?"

"He's got my cell phone on him. 301-258-5512."

"Thanks. Let me give him a call." I watched Dr. Daniel set the transducer down onto the portable ultrasound machine and take off his gloves. Dumping them into the trash, he quickly washed his hands in the sink that was next to my bed. He then picked up the hospital phone and dialed my cell. My heart had now made her way into my dry throat.

"...yes, this is Dr. Daniel...Hey man, how are you?...I'm doing well, thanks...So, I'm here with Megan, and as I explained to her, the baby is not doing well...yes, that's right, sir. So what we need to do is probably take the baby now because he's infected with Chorioamnionitis. His heart rate is not good. But I have two patients that I'm concerned with, and they are your girlfriend and the baby...Yes, that's what they both have. They both have Chorioamnionitis. So I want to know if you'd prefer us to do a C-section or wait another day for the baby to hit 24 weeks. If he's able to make it to at least that, his chances will be a little better...Okay, sir. Thanks."

Dr. Daniel pressed the END button and laid the phone on the bed. "So Mateo says that he wants the C-section." He kept his eyes on me as he waited for me to concur. A few seconds later, he donned another set of blue gloves and picked the transducer back up, slathering the warm gel across my belly once more. He resumed watching the baby again on the screen. I licked my parched lips and began to think quickly as my heart now thudded inside my ears, demanding an answer to this madness, as well. As soon as I parted my lips to give him the go-ahead to do the operation, Dr. Daniel stopped moving his hand and looked at me apologetically.

"I'm sorry, but your baby's heart has stopped beating."

• • •

I was given pitocin to induce labor. Sydney, the nurse on duty, offered me pain medicine. But I refused it as a punishment for not being able to keep this baby safe inside of me. I told myself that I had to suffer through the pain because I was a bad mom and a bad person, and I had failed my sons—not just the son inside of me, but the one who died in infancy a year before...and the one who was at home now, eagerly waiting for me to bring home his (live) brother.

And then there was Mateo. God, he was going to be so upset with me for losing yet another one of his children. As I sat in the silent and eerily lonely labor room, my mind traveled back to last summer, and how Mateo's mere pushes and slaps suddenly graduated to chokes and punches once he started blaming me for baby Isaiah's sudden death. Now, I was *petrified* at the thought of having to face him; that's why I never even called to tell him that Junior— we were going to name the baby after him—had passed before he was even born. I was hoping that the doctors would tell him for me.

I sat there in pain for three hours until my body was ready to eject the awful thing that took up residence inside of me. When I finally felt the uncontrollable urge to push, I let out an embarrassing *Help!* because I was terrified to give birth to a dead baby. Sydney ran into my room seconds later—panting, but patient and understanding—and held onto my hand as we waited for Dr. Daniel to come back and deliver my dead son.

"Would you like a priest to come in?"

I nodded my head quickly and gratefully, giving Sydney the best smile I could muster. "Yes please."

She returned the smile and held my gaze. Her genuine sympathy caused my eyes to water again. "Sure. Is there anything else I can do for you before I leave?"

I sniffled and shook my head. "No thanks. But thank you for being so nice to me."

• • •

"God took my baby because I'm a bad mother." Those were the first words I said to the priest when he replaced nurse Sydney and sat down by my bedside. From the side of my right eye, I saw him raise his eyes and nervously adjust the white band of his religious collar, visibly shocked by my statement.

He recovered quickly, however, gaining back his composure by clearing his throat. He spoke calmly. "Now, why do you think you're a bad mother?"

I kept my eyes towards the white ceiling. I lost another baby, so I *must* be a bad mother." I stopped and took a slow breath because the tears were beginning to drown my throat once again. I used both hands to wipe the sides of my face. I then turned my body slowly to my right, ever so carefully, because the baby's umbilical cord still rested between my legs, attached to a placenta that wasn't yet ready to leave my otherwise empty uterus. I had to wait for my tired body to find the strength to summon one more, final contraction to rid myself of the rest of this nightmare. This was my punishment for going back to Mateo, even after God had given me a way out.

I looked up at the priest. I assumed him to be just a little older than my 26 years—too young, in my opinion, to decide so early that he wanted to commit his whole life to the priesthood. But I was glad for the peace that he shared with me during that horrible moment. "Because I have one kid...and I should've learned *then*. God says premarital sex is a no-no..." I chuckled at myself. "But I never learn because I always try to force things to be, as if *I* have control over everything and *everybody* that I want in life."

I stopped as a small contraction took hold of my mid-section. I wondered if the placenta was finally ready to leave my body and thought about calling for Sydney to come back in. But I felt no need to push and the contraction just as soon faded. I moved my body back to the center of the bed and looked at the ceiling once more, as I wondered what I was going to tell Caleb when he asked about his baby brother.

"You seem to be very hard on yourself." I was able to see the priest smile before he inched his chair a little closer to the bed and placed both elbows onto his thin knees, folding his hands as if in prayer so that he could rest his small chin. "We don't know that God wanted this for you. We don't know that God is so-called punishing you, as you say. Sometimes, we just...don't know."

I nodded.

The priest continued softly. "What exactly scares you right now?"

I blinked. It was an odd question, but one I surprisingly had an answer to. I looked over at the priest as a gentle ray of light came in through the window, filling the room with a warm glow. And that's when I knew God had forgiven me for whatever sins that led me up to this very point.

My lips trembled. "My baby's father. I'm scared of *him* because I lost another baby."

• • •

Mateo arrived an hour after I finally passed the placenta. He asked if I had the C-section yet, not realizing that Junior had already passed, and that his still body rested just beyond the light blue curtain that kept nurse Sydney hidden from view as she bathed and clothed the baby, preparing him for us to finally meet him.

• • •

I was left with useless breastmilk and a now-misshapen belly after leaving Junior's sweet, little body at the hospital for cremation.

I felt like a waste of a woman because I could not give birth to healthy babies. I found no value in being Caleb's mother, or being a straight-A student in college...or even being a stellar employee at the hospital—the one who deeply loved her patients, who could also insert an IV into *any* vein. No, my entire worth was tied into cementing my relationship with Mateo and making him a father so that I could make an instant family and belong to *somebody*. However, once I got home from the hospital two days after Junior passed, Mateo didn't seem to care as much about the death of *this child* like he did when our first baby had passed 11 months ago. I was grateful for this because it would spare me the physical anger I became victim to when Mateo had come to the conclusion that I was the reason Isaiah died.

• • •

"Mateo!" I yelled for him one afternoon from the guest bathroom of his father's house. Because I would be out of work for "maternity leave," (and because Mateo had never really helped with the rent, anyway), I had lost the *second* apartment I had worked so hard to get. Mateo's father had felt sorry for us and let us move in with him. "Mateo, could you come in here please?"

He showed up seconds later, a little out of breath from running up the basement staircase. "Yeah, Megan, what's wrong?"

"My breasts are leaking, see?" I pulled my blouse open and gestured towards the trail of breastmilk that was beginning to make its way from my nipples down to my still-swollen belly. The milk resembled the color of egg whites, and my eyes began to tear as I realized how unfair life was.

Mateo took a moment to answer. His hand propped against the frame of the bathroom, he looked down at my breasts and then back up at me before casually shrugging his shoulders. "Well,

Megan, you're gonna have that—"

"—*what*—?"

"—I mean what did you expect? You *just* had another baby—"

"—but...but—?"

"—but, you're gonna have that, *Megan*." I watched in disbelief as he dropped his hand from the door frame and gave another hunch of his dark shoulders. He made a step towards me. "Now, come on. Lemme help you button this shirt back up before Caleb walks in and sees you."

I was silent as I let the father of my two dead babies button up my shirt as if I were a child, wincing as his hand absentmindedly brushed against my full breasts in an effort to latch the two top buttons. When he was finished, he bent down and gave me a quick peck on my forehead. Immediately, I smelled the scent of Tommy Hiflfiger's *True Star Men* as he lifted his lips from me.

"Why are you wearing cologne?"

"Huh? What?"

"You just got back from work—why did you just put cologne on?"

His sharp eyes skittered to and fro as he thought of an answer. "Because it's hot outside, and I'm about to go back out—"

"—back *out*—?'

"—yeah, back out because I got some things to do with my cousin real quick—"

"—and what does that have to do with your putting cologne on?"

He blew out an exasperated breath, clearly irritated with me but trying hard not to show it. "Because, *Megan*, it's hot as shit outside and when I sweat, I don't want to smell bad." He hunched his shoulders again and motioned with his head. "Now c'mon. I already helped Caleb with his homework, and I'm only gonna be gone for a couple of hours."

I felt confused and alone.

• • •

I found out about the other woman in Mateo's life two months after we lost Junior. Curiosity got the best of me one afternoon while Caleb was at school, Mateo was at work, and the only thing left to keep me company was my mounting depression. I probably had no business answering Mateo's father's house phone, but Mr. James had made it clear to me that his house was *my* house as long as I needed it, and since the phone rang for the fourth time in fifteen minutes with *Shannon Bernard* displayed on the caller ID, I figured it could have been an emergency...

"Hello?"

"Um...hello?"

"Yes...hello? Who are you looking for?"

"I'm looking for Mateo. Is he there?"

"Um, no, Mateo isn't here." I pulled the cordless from my ear and looked at the caller ID again. Who was Shannon Bernard? Mateo had never mentioned her before. "Who are you and how do you know Mateo?"

"Oh! Well I'm Shannon. You must be Mateo's cousin.."

I cleared my throat. "His cousin...?"

"Yeah! His cousin Me—"

"—I'm not his cousin. I'm his *girlfriend*."

The conversation suddenly stopped as she and I took a few moments to process what was going on. My heart began thudding inside her ribcage as my mind searched wildly for any reasonable answer as to why Mateo would call me his *cousin*. When I finally found the courage to open my mouth and ask, Shannon beat me to it.

"Didn't you used to live off Branch Avenue, by the Air Force base...?"

I nodded inside the quiet of that kitchen, as if she could actually see me, and gave a cautious *yes*.

"And wasn't there a Shell gas station right across the street from your apartment...?"

My eyebrows immediately met in the middle in confusion as my brain worked furiously to figure out who *Shannon Bernard* was. "There was," I heard myself say into the mouthpiece."

There was another pause before Shannon said, "So you must have been the pregnant cousin—?"

"—the pregnant *cousin*...??"

She gave a loud and frustrated sigh and her voice seemed to shake when she responded next. "Mateo had dropped a folded sonogram inside my apartment one morning before leaving, and your name was on the front." *Pause.* "He told me you were his *cousin*."

And suddenly, I understood why Junior's death wasn't affecting Mateo as badly as Isaiah's had almost a year ago.

I managed to swallow the growing swelling inside my throat and quietly asked Shannon, "how long?"

"W-w-what?"

I blinked back the tears that began to gather at the corners of my eyes and asked a little louder, "How long have you...how long have you and Mateo been seeing each other?" But I really didn't want to know the answer.

She hesitated from the other end of the line as I imagined her wrestling with whether or not she should answer my question and betray Mateo's trust. After all, she owed me nothing. Out of nowhere, I wondered if Mateo put his hands on her, like he did to me.

"Two years."

"*Two years?*"

"Yes."

I didn't respond. We remained quiet from our respective ends of the phone as we silently made sense of what had been going on right underneath our noses. As tears wet my cheeks my mind traveled back to all the nights I stayed up waiting on Mateo to come home from work...to the several occasions he flew out of our apartment during an argument and I wouldn't see him for days...and to the night I had given birth to our first son, Isaiah, just to see him disappear shortly after he made sure the baby and I were stable after delivery:

Wait a minute—you're not leaving, are you?

Megan, I can't stay. He had sounded impatient, as if I should've already known that fact. *I have to work tomorrow and I don't know how to get to work from here.*

Bullshit. Really? Mateo had grown up in D.C., and he certainly spent nearly all his free time there, especially when he was out past midnight *every fucking day*. For Chrissakes, we were already *in* D.C! We were already *in* the fucking city, and he didn't know how to get to work from where we were...???

But I had been too weak to argue because of the fever that ravaged my body, and too worried about Isaiah, who had been whisked to the NICU shortly before the nurses wheeled me to my recovery room. I watched Mateo leave that night, only to return three days later when I was discharged.

"Did you have the baby?"

"Huh?" I snapped back to the present scene inside of Mr. James's kitchen and wiped the warm tears from my face. "I'm sorry, what did you say?"

Shannon cleared her throat and hesitated before quietly

asking, "Did you have the baby?"

"Yes. But he was stillborn." It almost sounded as if Shannon blew out a very subtle sigh of relief, but I could've just imagined it.

"Oh! I'm sorry—"

"—it's fine. Thank you. But I should go now." I clicked the *OFF* button without waiting for her to respond and placed the phone back into its cradle on the wall. My pregnancy was over. Junior was gone. I had to withdraw from my classes at the community college for a moment while I fought through my depression...and Mateo had already moved on, courtesy of *Shannon Bernard*. I slumped to the floor in quiet tears as the puzzle pieces began to expertly float together, constructing the actual reality that should have already been clear to me: Mateo's late-nights out, the moments he spent more than 24 hours away from home, and now his eagerness to proceed with his life as if Junior never existed... it all had to do with another woman.

My shirt suddenly felt moist, and I immediately looked down to see two small puddles spreading where the blouse covered my nipples. I gave a swipe of my eyes and stood. I traveled to the bedroom Mateo and I shared, slowly popped my Celexa and Ativan, and just...stared off into black space... letting the drugs flood any feelings I may have had, temporarily.

17

Ian

"Goodnight"

Sometimes,
I wish I had
never met you.
Then I would
never know the
heartache of loving
you, only to
have it returned
to me in
my dreams.

It was a pain to move again, but having to temporarily drop out of
school, lose two babies back to back, and find out that the father
of those two babies had successfully lived another life completely
unbeknownst to me—*while I had ridiculously laid down my life
and all but burned my soul for him*—had *finally* become more than
I could bear. *Finally.*

The day I couldn't even make it out of bed to take Caleb to

177

school and thus, had him dress himself *and* walk himself five minutes to the building, alone, at *six years of age,* was the time I realized I couldn't continue the life I was living.

I wanted to die. I wanted to close my eyes and never wake up. That was the only solution *I* could see...because I was so caught up in this nasty web of deception and heartache, spun with a double dose of my own stupidity, that I couldn't see *any fucking way out of.*

And then the antidepressants–

Half the time I was so doped up on dopamine, serotonin, and the rest of the happy, manufactured neurotoxins. My brain was so scrambled with the influx of chemicals that I remained a fucking zombie for more than eight hours out of the day. And when I was alert and coherent, I had this relentless headache and the constant nausea. The only thing I could do was sit and stare...

I couldn't even mourn the death of my child because there were things to do that were more important, like *FIGURING OUT A WAY OF FINALLY GETTING OUT OF THIS FUCKING PRISON CELL.*

I was so far in, and I'm ashamed to tell you how deep that hole was for me.

Mateo had changed a little by the time we lost Junior, and he was taking better care of Caleb, and with the help of his father, Mr. James, I was actually living in better than normal circumstances. Yes, I had dropped out of school, but Mr. James didn't take rent from me. In fact, he took *no money* from me. And when I worked on Fridays at the hospital, he or Mateo, would pick "the grandson" (that's what he called Caleb) up from aftercare, which was, very conveniently so, located one block down from his house.

But after that conversation with *Shannon Bernard*–

I stupidly couldn't take Mateo's disrespect anymore. I always knew he didn't love me, but the blatant disrespect he was now able to give me because we were at his *father's house, and* he had his free-dom...? I didn't have the mental capacity to take it anymore

I used to look back and ask myself if I could press *Rewind*, would I have decided to remain at Mr. James's house instead? Would I have finally found a way to turn off feelings that had proved irrelevant to my life, and just *take it*—in return for free housing, free food, and free child care? Would I have decided to put myself aside, instead of making the decision to move *again*, on a whim...?

I'm not sure. It was an impossible situation. Either I stayed and lost whatever mental faculty I had left while pretending I no longer existed, or I lived with a young woman I barely knew—a *coworker*, no less—who had found the perfect opportunity to exploit my pathetic circumstances. I no longer had Kelly to help me clean up my messes. When I had called her the day I found out about *Shannen Bernard*, she exhaled a breath of frustration mixed and annoyance, and cooly told me:

I'm sorry Megan, but I can't support you anymore with all the drama you continue to keep with Mateo. You knew he was bad for you all along; this shouldn't be a surprise for you. And yet, you kept going back.

And with that, she ceased taking my calls.

I wasn't smart back then. I wasn't practical. And even after moving in with the roommate from work, I continued repeating my mistakes by sleeping with Mateo off and on. My rationale? Because he was still helping me out with Caleb during the week-ends when I worked. No, we were no longer together, a fact he made sure I understood once he was finally off the hook, guaran-teed by my departure from his father's house. But I persisted in the game of *pretend*, tricking myself into believing Mateo really was mine forever. As long as he maintained *some kind of presence* in my life, *that* was enough for me.

I knew what love was. But I had learned over the years that I was not good enough to receive this *love*. So I took what I could get, choosing to settle because I *could not take* being alone.

But before I had agreed to accompany Mateo down to the innermost depths of depravity, I *did still believe* I was capable of striving for this *true love* that was decent, kind, smart, and loyal... even after Adam had abandoned Caleb and me.

• • •

A few weeks after I'd settled into The Guadalupe Home October of 1998, I was allowed to travel back to Austin for a weekend pass at my father's. On that Saturday night, I went out with Tamron's niece Alaya, and after the club closed we found ourselves moseying through the still-lively, 5th street atmosphere at midnight. Ahead of us was a young man and woman, and I noticed that the man kept pausing his steps to look back at me. Finally he stopped, and bravely walked towards me and Alaya and told me:

I just wanted to tell you that you are so beautiful.

Huh??? I was about three months pregnant, though no one would ever know because I was barely 110 pounds at that time, so there was no baby poking through my belly just yet. But *I* knew I was pregnant and abandoned at the age of eighteen, so I felt ugly and discarded. I tried my best, however, to disguise how I felt on a regular basis, and I was presently in a light blue, skinny, mini-dress, something I'd worn for Adam once when we were in love for that very short period of time. Snug in the middle, but still not betraying the fact that I carried a life inside of me.

I was shocked, especially since he seemed to have his girlfriend right next to him. I asked him politely, *But aren't you with her?*

His perfectly carved face broke into a smile and he shook his head back and chuckled lightly, his black curls bouncing in the moonlight. *Who? Her? Noooo, that's my sister.*

A symphony of laughs from him, his sister–who'd reached out her hand to say *Nice to meet you*–and eventually, me and Alaya.

I got his number but never gave him mine, as I had *no number* of my own since the phone at the shelter was a group phone, shared between the house mother, me, and the rest of the girls at the residence. After returning to The Guadalupe Home, I waited a week before finally gathering enough courage to call and tell him that I didn't have my own number...that I was pregnant, on my own, and living in a home that nuns used to inhabit (no pun intended).

He was pensive, but a week later he called me. And then *that* phone call turned into weekly phone calls from his naval station in San Diego. Phone calls then turned into routine hand-written letters exchanged between us. When he went away on the aircraft carrier for six months, I wasn't able to hear his voice for the duration. But he made sure to send postcards from each country he docked at, complete with a little note that always ended with *Miss you.*

This lasted until I left The Guadalupe Home and found myself in my little apartment in San Antonio, trying my best to keep my nose above water with baby Caleb dog-peddling by my side. When New Years of 2000 came, my pen pal drove from his family's home, which he had been visiting for Christmas in Killeen, Texas, and finally came to see me for the first time since we'd met a little over a year before.

It was great. Texas was warm for the holidays, so I was able to dress in a little winter "sundress," if you will, while Caleb was clothed in a blue onesie with matching shorts. My pen pal took us out to eat at this swanky Chinese restaurant not too far from my place, and then we headed back to my cozy apartment, baked chocolate chip cookies, and put Caleb to bed.

We celebrated the new year wrapped in each other's arms all night. He got the sex, and by the time he made it back to his duty station in California a few days later, I received one of his regular hand-written letters, thanking me for a good time but letting me know that he wasn't ready for a relationship.

Instant. Balloon. POP. And he couldn't have decided that *before* he fucked me?

We still kept in touch, but it wasn't the same. I felt used and dumb, and there was no way I could go back to being just *friends*, not after the year and a half we spent building a bond over time and distance that I thought was sure to hold for years to come. For Valentine's Day he sent me a skimpy pink ensemble from *Victoria's Secret*, but it wound up in the back of my underwear drawer somewhere, never to be found again until I gave up my apartment to go to Basic Training for the military. After a few months, I grew tired of receiving his letters, his words starting to feel forced, contrived, orchestrated...guilty. And I just stopped responding.

I threw away all his dishonest love notes, but kept his postcards and the one picture he sent me in his Navy blues. After all, the postcards were still beautiful to me—tangible reminders of precious memories that I didn't mind keeping tucked away in the hidden compartments of my mind.

For a moment, I was able to enjoy the fantasy that I had finally captured this "true love" in my pen pal. I imagined him uncovering my worth and potential, even underneath the *single mom* brand.

And then came Ian Green, about ten months after receiving my *Dear Jane* letter from the Navy seaman. And, in true Megan fashion, I tried *again* to attain the love that continued to elude me. I had wanted so badly to be *the one* for him. It wasn't just for his (also) perfectly chiseled dark face, his low, mysterious voice, and the Haitian accent he used *oh-so-very* sexily when he was teaching me French while making love to me. It was because he owned a brilliant mind, and we were able to convene and exchange ideas about our visionary works in progress. It was because we enjoyed each other's company at movies, dinners, even Mass. We could've gone to a monastery together for a silent, weekend retreat, enveloped in one another's love while basking in the peace God offers... and we would've been *happy*.

Ian held my attention captive. He was a quiet genius who spoke English, French, *and* Haitian Creole fluently. The little bit of Spanish he thought he knew, I was able to supplement with my own lessons tailored just for him. There wasn't a subject on this planet that he didn't know at least a little bit about, so there was never a shortage of conversation between us. I was able to learn from him, and he from me. We could talk to one another through our eyes, our body language, our *stillness*. He understood my passion for learning, creating, and just *living*. And because of his hard work and ambition, I knew he would one day make a decent husband and a wonderful father to his children since he came from a family that loved him dearly. Oh, how I had wanted *so badly* to be a part of that one day. He had completed me, and I *him*.

And then I had the abortion.

And then I conceived our only child in the warm glow of a Saturday evening, following his sister's Communion. We had rushed back to the apartment because he couldn't stand to keep his hands away from me for *not one more second* after watching me (subtly) sway my hips to and fro every chance I got while inside the sacred church. I was wearing the short, yellow sundress I knew would turn him savage, complemented by the tall yellow wedges that heightened my confidence. But I was suffering severely from anxiety, which had yet to be diagnosed. I was raising Caleb by myself while battling with my mental decline and trying to be this *amazing* young mother against all the opposition that said I couldn't. So I had inadvertently made Ian my crutch, my strength, my sanctuary. I needed him to be in my presence *at all times*, to be able to rely on him for everything I couldn't bear on my own, even though we were only twenty-two years old. Not having him by my side to give me the constant attention and reassurance I continued to seek made me feel like I had done something wrong...like I was being punished for being a single mom...like it was Adam leaving Caleb and me all over again. And that feeling I *could not take.*

Looking back, he had tried his best to love me the way I needed. But he knew I wasn't in his future... and deep, deep down, *I* knew it, too. Having that second abortion only succeeded in finally pushing me off the steep slope I had already been hanging onto, dropping me into the center of the black hole that I thought I had escaped forever. But getting me pregnant also made him realize that his need to marry a woman with strong familial ties and no previous children was greater than any love he may have felt for me, and that was just *life*. Nothing personal, just business. I had been a mental basket-case, had the kid out of wedlock, and with barely any family nearby and an absentee child's father, I was basically a ward of the state looking for anyone to adopt me and my child. And Ian and I were *only twenty-two years old.*

I was a nontraditional woman who wanted a traditional relationship. That's why I try so hard, against the odds, to prove my worth.

Looking back... no, I couldn't blame him for moving on.

• • •

"Soooo...are we gonna go back to your place...?"

But I *could* blame him for returning.

I blinked away my random thoughts and refocused my

attention on Ian, a little miffed by his desire to go to the apartment I was sharing with Lauren. "*My* place? I thought you may wanna grab something to eat. I mean, it's been like, four years since I last saw you..."

"Megan, it's in the middle of the day, and I'm sure it's lunch hour, and then the traffic is gonna start... Let's just go to your place."

I didn't approve, but told him *Okay* and put my car in gear, leaving the freshly painted curb of Ian's parents' new home in the sweet suburbs of Laurel. Apparently, they had purchased the home about a year after Ian left me in Maryland to go pursue his military career in New Jersey.

I was pensive on the 25-minute drive back to my place, thankful for the moderate traffic on the highway that kept my attention on the road and away from my passenger. I had been beyond excited when I got his phone call two days before to tell me he'd be in town to visit his parents. Like, *heart-leaping-out-of-my-fucking-chest* excited. But now I tread cautiously since I knew that he was set to get married soon, if he weren't already...

(I shot a quick glance downwards towards his left ring finger. No ring yet.)

So, then, *what the hell was I even doing with him?* I couldn't tell you. Maybe I needed my ego stroked, or maybe I was just wishing for a miracle that his past four years *post- Megan break up* was just a mistake, he realized, and he was coming back for me...?

"So *why* did you want to meet up again? I mean, I'm thrilled to see you, but aren't you—"

"—what..?"

I knew he had heard me, but I turned my eyes back to the road when the traffic light turned green. I didn't want to start an argument, especially when his whole mood exuded conflict, indifference, and frustration all at once. All that was needed was the wrong word from me to ignite his fire, the fire he and I *both* shared deep inside of us. I let out a quiet sigh of frustration myself, suddenly wondering why I was even in the same car as him in the first place after all that had happened between us.

• • •

"So this is where you live now...?"

I straightened my little white Nissan between the painted white lines and put it in park. "This is where *my coworker* and I live, but she's at work." I removed the keys from the ignition and opened my side. "Come on, let's go."

Ian followed suit, slowly making his way through the apartment once I unlocked the front door, meticulously eyeing everything there was to see. After a minute or two, he paused at a framed picture of Caleb that furnished the cream-colored bar.

"This is Caleb now?"

His voice was low, but it echoed inside the small apartment since Lauren and I barely had any furniture. I was quiet for a moment as I watched his long fingers graze the top of the wooden frame, remembering days past when those same slender fingers used to graze my own body.

"Yeah, that's him. He's seven now." Caleb was just three the last time Ian saw him.

"Where is he now?"

I raised an eyebrow, completely surprised that he cared enough to ask. "Well, he's actually visiting my father in Texas. I'm taking classes this summer and needed the help—"

"—ah, yes...your classes." Ian gently placed Caleb's picture back on the counter. "What classes are you taking?"

Goosebumps populated my bare arms as I opened my mouth

and got ready to talk about one of my favorite subjects, still so grateful that God had opened a way for me to go back to college after I had left Mr. James's place. "Um, a couple of English classes and a sociology course. I love this school shit, you know."

"Yes, you're beaming now."

I felt the slight red spread across my face, and I turned my head towards the kitchen so that he wouldn't see the effect he still had on me, four years later. But it didn't take me long to recover after I reminded myself that I had seen somewhere on my Facebook feed that Ian was now engaged, or he had already gotten married, one of the two...

"So where is...*he*?"

I snapped my head back towards Ian. "He...*who*?"

"Your *boyfriend*..."

"If I had a boyfriend, you wouldn't be here..."

"Megan..." I watched as Ian shifted his weight from one foot to the other, propping one elbow onto the bar, blowing out that annoying puff of air he had grown accustomed to blowing when I was pregnant with his child, several lifetimes ago. "You know what I mean."

"His name is *Mateo*, and I guess he would be *at work*. And, he's not my *boyfriend*. That's been over for a while now."

"Yeah, right."

"I'm sorry... ?" I had heard him, but wanted to make sure I had heard right, hotly wondering for a quick moment what business it was of his when he had left me to fend for myself after ordering me out of the apartment...after the abortion. How could he expect complete transparency from me when he couldn't be honest with himself–?

"Nothing." He looked... defeated.

The sudden silence and past memories were more than I could

handle. I offered him a *Corona* and we sat on the sofa, he on one end, me safely on the other. We remained quiet for a long while as, I'm sure, he tried to process the life I had made after he left to flourish in the sunrise, wondering if he had made the right decision four or five years ago to walk away.

But then the abortion happened–

That fucking abortion...

–followed by the depression and anxiety that threatened to swallow me whole.

I had been too much of a situation, for *anybody*.

I cleared my throat and crossed one leg over the other, while smoothing out the pink fabric of my dress over my knee. Yes, of course he had made the right decision. He could tell just by looking around the nearly empty, two-bedroom apartment, with the one bedroom in the back that I shared with my seven-year old son.

I pulled in a deep breath before those fucking tears hit the fronts of my eyeballs, wishing for some kind of internal drought to temporarily dry out my emotional lake. I took a sip of my beer, breaking the silence with a refreshing giggle as a distant memory came to chase the tears away.

"What's so funny?" I looked over towards my guest and suppressed a smile with my hand. His Adam's apple moved with the swallow of his beverage, and his tired eyes were focused and serious.

"It's nothing." I took another sip of my drink as I remembered how Ian had gone away, too, just like my pen pal had, for one month on the airship carrier (me and military men, right?). We had no contact with one another, except for the emails we were able to exchange every other day. I remembered how I had to use the computers during my breaks at the hospital, eager as a fresh teenager in love for the first time to read his sweet words to me (at the time, I didn't own my own computer). And when his ship finally docked in the U.S. and he was able to drive back home to Maryland, he had surprised me and Caleb with pizza and a dozen red roses when he finally made it back to our apartment.

I had tried hard to hold onto the one person who I *knew* could love me and Caleb the way we deserved. And he tried, *too*, but he had to fill shoes he wasn't quite ready to wear yet. Our relationship was doomed even before it had started.

Why did life have to be so sad?

"Megan...*Sunny*...I..."

His dark face was suddenly against mine, and wisps of my hair were softly entangled inside the lithe fingers of his hand. His former nickname for me paused my breathing and halted my heartbeat. I could feel his familiar air as he lightly rested his weary forehead against mine and slowly blew out his discontent and uncertainty.

Why couldn't he have just waited for me to get my shit together? I was working on it. It was a process. All I needed was for him to have a little faith and patience...

"Megan..."

I said nothing because I remembered that he was supposed to be married, or was *about to be* married, and that even though I loved him from the depths of my soul, my love (infatuation) for Mateo trumped all people...because Mateo was *there*. There with me in the state of Maryland, no matter how violent our relationship had been—not somewhere, living in New Jersey, about to get married to someone who wasn't *me*.

How could Ian be so cruel to come back and play this evil trick on me?

Ian pulled my lips closer to his with the gentle tug of my hair, and if I could, I would've given the world for the chance to be his all over again. But I didn't understand what this was all about... what his coming to my place was all about...what his *touch* was all about. I just didn't understand, and I didn't want to trick myself into believing that this could be attainable love, all over again.

So I pulled back, wiped away a regretful tear, and stood. I told him we had to go. He was reluctant, but complied. After quietly following me back to my little white Nissan, I dropped him back off to the other side of the world... to his parents' beautiful home... to a life I would never be a part of.

No more *unicorns and fairy dust.*

18

Let Go

"I know that you're pregnant. But he told me that he's just going to be there for the *baby*, and that's it." Shannon Bernard's voice echoed inside my ears as my nurse searched my arm for a vein. God, I was getting so sick and tired of hearing that fucking line, as her words yanked me back to eight years before, when Caleb's father had made the same statement to me. You have sex unprotected, wind up pregnant, and suddenly, you don't exist anymore...as if your getting knocked up had everything to do with *you*, and nothing to do with the other party. Except Adam never made good on his promise, and for some reason, even though Mateo had played me *and* Shannon at the same time for the past few years, I somehow knew that he was going to be there for our child.

"Okay, you ready? I found a vein." That was my nurse, Jackie, who chuckled as she gently tapped the vein she was eyeing . "You don't have too many of them, but I found one good one."

I nodded and gave my nurse a smile. "Sure, no problem." I drew in a long breath as Jackie inserted her needle and guided it through the skin of my forearm. Shannon's reality check came when I was five months pregnant with Mateo's third child, after I had come home to find her sitting in her car as she waited for

Mateo to gather three months' worth of belongings from the new apartment Mateo's father had ended up renting for me.

"You're all done! Now, does this hurt?" I waited as Jackie flushed the cool saline through my new line to double-check that she was still in the vein.

I gave a quick shake of my head. "No, it's fine. Thank you."

"Good. And now I'm also gonna place this cannula inside your nose, just to give you a boost of oxygen."

"Okay." I breathed again, thankful for the extra air, though the sudden need for it made me wonder if I was going to survive the preeclampsia.

"So Jackie, you sure the C-section is necessary? What I mean is, we can't try and wait to see if she can just push him out?" That was Mateo, who was seated to my left, waist bent as both his steady elbows rested on his knees. The black fitted *DC* cap that he wore cast a dark but handsome shadow across his eyes.

"Um, yeah...it is." Jackie finished looping the plastic tubing over the tops of my ears and glanced at Mateo. "She's pre-eclamptic. Her blood pressure is rising and she's not dilating fast enough, so we need to get the little one out as quickly as we can..."

I gave a subtle roll of my eyes towards a God who had to be done with me by now. So nice of Mateo to care at this point in time after abandoning me half-way into the pregnancy, having Shannon bring him to my apartment when he thought I would still be at work. *What a sneaky ass coward.* I wanted to laugh out loud as the *Dinamap* machine began to squeeze my arm for another pressure reading while Mateo and Jackie discussed my impending Cesarean. No matter how terrible we were for one another, no matter what Mateo did to me, all he ever had to do was knock on my door, find my soul with his dark eyes, and I was his all over again. The only thing that ever mattered to me was the present—the here and now in which Mateo wanted and needed me all over again. Not our disastrous past, not a very unpredictable future, not the fact that I had lost Kelly as a friend when she finally tired of the shit I kept maintaining with Mateo, and *certainly* not the two years in school that I just completed towards my associate's degree while building a life free from drama for both me *and* Caleb, *while* keeping a perfect gpa. I continued to watch Mateo as he easily engaged Jackie in conversation as if he didn't have a care in the world...as if he didn't have Shannon on standby, waiting as patiently as she could stand it to find out whether or not the birth of our baby would suddenly glue us together as a family. But the distance that he kept from me as he sat in a chair by the corner, away from my hospital bed, subtly showed that that was never going to happen. However, I was glad he was there for me—I mean, for *the baby*.

• • •

Baby Benjamin was safely pulled from me in the early afternoon hours the day after Christmas. At 8lbs, he was a chunky, healthy size—a bittersweet reminder of his two older brothers who never saw the outside of the hospital, who had both been able to fit inside just the palm of one hand. Mateo was the first one to hold our son since both of my arms were restrained during the surgery. Watching him cradle the baby protectively against his chest, I caught a tear rolling down the side of his face.

• • •

Mateo left shortly after the surgeons sewed my belly back together, checked little Benjamin's APGAR scores, and wheeled me to my room. There was a comfortable recliner in the corner of my new room for dads to sleep in with mom and baby, but, fortunately for Shannon, baby Benjamin would not be the miracle adhesive that would bind Mateo and me together again. In the dark of that room, with just the newborn scent of Benjamin cuddled close to my breasts, I realized that God had only been trying to warn me when I lost little Isaiah *and* Junior.

• • •

Mateo never came back to visit me and his son during the two days we spent isolated with one another in our hospital room. Thankfully, my sister Avery came to visit us on the day of our discharge. She drove us to Target so she could buy whatever I needed for the baby, and then she took us back home and set up the crib and the Winnie-the-Pooh swing before she left. I was grateful for her, as the only thing I could do was hold the baby carefully in my arms while sitting close to his aunt, the C-section making it almost impossible for me to move around.

"So it looks like everything is set up for little Benjamin." Avery blew out a breath and wiped her brow, obviously worn from putting Benjamin's crib together. "Are you going to be okay?"

"Yeah, I'm okay. Thank you again for everything!" I nodded quickly in an effort to convince both her and myself that Benjamin and I were going to be just fine in the apartment by ourselves, and that Mateo's absence meant nothing to me.

• • •

Caleb wasn't present for the birth of his brother. As soon as schools let out for the Christmas break, he had flown down south to enjoy the Florida sun at his grandmother's new house, a project Veronica had built from the ground up when she retired a couple of years before. I was glad Caleb got a vacation away from the chaos that I continued to create in my life. Thank God I had gone into labor while he was gone; it had saved me from having to search for someone to stay with him while Benjamin and I were in the hospital.

• • •

Once Caleb finally arrived at BWI airport, and after we had made it home, I found Mateo in the living room seated on the same leather sofa he had brought to my apartment months ago when I first found out I was pregnant with Benjamin—when he believed he wanted to start over with me, Caleb and the new baby. After the lease was up at the last apartment, Lauren and I parted ways (Lauren had also transferred to another unit in the hospital), and I did not have the income required to get a place of my own. Thank God I had still maintained a relationship with Mr. James, though, who had leased my new apartment for just Caleb and me.

Holding his son in his arms, Mateo kept his head snuggled close to Benjamin's while Benjamin slept soundly.

I softly told Mateo *Hey* but he kept his head down and barely whispered *What's up*. Didn't even look up when Caleb entered the room, even though he hadn't seen him in weeks. He was on his *I-can't-stand-Megan*-shit again, almost as if he wished he could make me disappear forever since he finally got his healthy baby. I closed my eyes momentarily, wishing that I could turn back the hands of time to at least two years back, hating myself for undoing every bit of progress I had made since Junior died by letting Mateo back in, unprotected.

Be careful what you wish for.

Five painful minutes passed before Mateo remembered his manners and said, *What's up, Caleb* to my oldest child. He still kept his head low, however, as if Caleb and I had done something wrong. The tension was suffocatingly thick, and I felt sorry that

Mateo was, once again, treating my son with so much shade, just as he had done when we all lived together two years ago, when I was pregnant with Junior. *If Mateo hated me so much, why did he keep making babies with me?* Taking a step towards the sofa, I tried to ease the awkwardness by introducing Caleb to his little brother.

"Come meet your new brother, Caleb." I gently placed my hands on Caleb's small shoulders and guided him towards Mateo and the baby.

Caleb walked carefully to the sofa where Mateo sat and tried to take a peek at his brother. Mateo wouldn't budge at first, keeping his head down and nuzzled next to his son's cheek. But after a few seconds of watching Caleb struggle, he finally relented, and turned the sleeping baby so that Caleb could finally see his face. God, he was such a jerk.

A few silent moments later, Mateo carefully stood and carried Benjamin to his bassinet and laid him down. Then he was out the door. Since bringing my son home from the hospital, Mateo's routine was to let himself into the apartment around 6 p.m. (with the key he still held onto that he felt entitled to keep since he was paying half my rent since I got pregnant), greet the baby, feed him, change him, and then put him down to sleep. All of this he did in complete silence while I tried my best to stay out of the way and pretend as if my heart weren't shattering into a gazillion fragile pieces when it came time for him to leave and go back home to *Shannon Bernard.*

• • •

Benjamin was two weeks old when Mateo told me his mother was in town and asked if it would be okay that she keep the baby for the weekend. I wasn't okay with my very new baby going anywhere outside of my apartment with people I didn't know. But I thought that giving Mrs. Baines the baby for a few days would gain her favor since she'd always been convinced that my being with Mateo was only a tactic for using him for whatever she thought he could provide for me and Caleb. Letting Benjamin go would be like a peace offering that would somehow bring us together.

I was fucking delusional, as always.

Mateo arrived at my place with his mother, her new husband, and an aunt I had never met. The whole 20 minutes that Mrs. Baines and her entourage sat in my living room, I never existed. She barely took a seat and barely said anything to me. Not even a hug or a *Congratulations Megan!* Couldn't even look me in the eye or even say, *Thank you Megan* for *welcoming me into your home and letting me take my grandson—even though you're breastfeeding, and I've never thought too much of you in the first place.* And the only interaction she had with Caleb was when she passed along a set of instructions for how to make Benjamin's tiny sample of infant formula explode by dropping a *Tums* inside the bottle.

Fucking bitch.

And with that, she, her entourage and her evil ass son were gone, along with my innocent baby. It was just me and Caleb left, all over again.

• • •

Then came the bullying. In the following weeks, Mateo would give a fifteen-minute "heads-up" and tell me that he was on his way to pick up his son. Using his key, he would open the door, collect the baby, and leave without letting me know when he was going to return him. One morning, after Caleb went to school, he even came over and raided my bedroom closet for Benjamin's clothes— clothes that *I* had bought for the baby—and threw them in a plastic trash bag and left in a hurry with his son. Another time, he *and* his brother, Shawn, had come to my house, demanding that I relinquish Benjamin to Mateo. It was a weeknight, Caleb was home, and Shawn stood guard and watched as Mateo literally wrestled Benjamin from my arms. And all Shawn could do was watch, wait, then grab the car seat—*my car seat*—after Mateo finally grabbed the baby from me. And because the Ironworkers had temporarily laid him off, he had all the time in the world to play these fucking games with me.

And every time he did this, I would call Constance (now the only friend left who could stand my continuous bullshit), and unload all my frustration.

"You know what, Megan?" She sounded concerned, but I could hint the aggravation in her voice. I wasn't sure if it was directed towards me or if the feeling was for Mateo, but she certainly sounded tired.

I breathed into the phone. I was tired, too. "Yes, Constance..."

"The next time Mateo comes for Benjamin, just let him take him..."

"*What???*" I was upset and confused. "But—"

"—just listen to me, Megan." And instantly, Constance's voice turned from one of annoyance to a tone of soothing. "Let Mateo take him, and say nothing. In fact, pack a bag for the baby and have it ready for him when he comes so that he doesn't have to go through your closet, or even come inside your house. He is not working right now, and has nothing better to do than to think of a million and one ways to piss you off. And it's working."

The next morning when Mateo arrived with his shit again, I was at the door, standing and waiting, with Benjamin in one arm and his diaper bag—complete with diapers, five changes of clothes, and wipes—in the other. He tried to conceal his surprise the best way he could, but he couldn't sustain his hardened face any longer when the only words I said to him were *Have a nice day.*

Later that afternoon, he called to say, "I'll be bringing Benjamin back in the morning."

It took a lot out of me to keep all the hateful words inside my mouth, choosing instead to mutter only, *Okay.*

• • •

But thankfully, Mateo had agreed to watch both Caleb and Benjamin on Saturdays and Sundays at the apartment when I went back to work at the hospital. But after the third weekend of coming home late from a long shift and watching Mateo immediately gather his things and walk out the door without so much as a *fuck you* to me, I couldn't take it anymore. He never spoke to me, never gave the baby a bath for the night, and never had the heart to stay for at least twenty minutes so that I could take my dirty scrubs off and get in the shower. Nope, I take that back: he *did* speak to me on one particular night. He appeared at the bathroom door while I was peeling off my uniform and told me that he thought Caleb had tried to burn Benjamin on purpose.

"Huh? What the hell are you *talking about*?"

"I asked him to warm the bottle for Benjamin and he made it too hot, *Megan.*"

I pulled off my scrub top and tossed it to the bathroom floor. "First of all, Mateo, why did Caleb even have to warm the bottle for you? What were you doing all damn day?" The anger deep inside me rose quickly as I continued to watch him fearlessly, as *he* began to lose his control, revealed by the pulsating vein in his dark forehead. He leaned closer to me, keeping his voice down.

"What the fuck do you mean, 'what was I doing all day'? Watching these damn kids. But *your son* warmed the fucking bottle too hot and I'm wondering if he did the shit on purpose..."

I moved in closer and met his hateful gaze. "You know damn well how much that boy loves Benjamin. He was only doing *you* a favor. And what the hell do you mean, *'your son'*? You're starting that *shit* again. He was 'your son' before Benjamin was born, and ever since then, you've been acting like a straight *asshole* when it comes to Caleb. Excuse me!" I moved around him to head out the bathroom because I knew where this was headed and wanted nothing to do with Mateo's misery. But he blocked me. When I tried to push my way through the door frame, he placed two fingers against my forehead and forced my head backwards. I snapped, slapping him across the face.

"Get the fuck out, Mateo! And from now on, you pick Benjamin up on Thursday nights and you bring him back Sunday nights when I get off from work. That way you won't have to worry about Caleb burning your poor, precious son!" I shoved past him this time, making sure to hurry to the living room where the kids were, knowing he wouldn't hit me while Caleb was watching. I glimpsed at my oldest son, who looked concerned. Benjamin continued to innocently babble from his spot inside his swing.

"And I need my key back, too," I barely whispered as my chest heaved. "Since you'll be keeping Benjamin for half of the week, I won't need your money to pay half of the rent. Therefore, you don't need any more access to my place."

Mateo remained quiet, and his own shame permeated the small living room as he fished through his pocket and removed his set of keys. He stared at me for a hard second before leaving the apartment. Didn't even say good-bye to *his* son.

"Thursday night, Mateo!" I managed to call out to him before he let the door slam behind him.

19

Stories

We all do what we have to do…

I started dreaming about Adam the year after I had given birth to Benjamin. Maybe it was due to the space finally freed inside my head since Mateo and I no longer kept relations outside of our son. The dreams were always the same: both Adam and I would be at his mother's house, located in Silver Spring, Maryland. The entire scene was always dark, the only light coming from a quiet TV located somewhere in the house. He and I would be in the same room, while his mother remained hidden somewhere inside the house. Nothing else would be going on, other than the fact that Adam and I were just…there. We'd never exchange words or even acknowledge one another's presence. And then, I would wake up.

Adam proved himself to be a coward during Caleb's childhood; the only thing he ever gave his son was the $150 I asked him for so that I could pay for our son's daycare tuition one week I couldn't afford it. And he didn't even want to wait until I got home to give it to me that evening. Instead, he took it to my mother's house where I was living at the time, and securely tucked it under the doormat. He called me to let me know it was there, and that was the last I heard from him. Caleb was two-years-old.

· · ·

I slowly breathed in the cedarwood scent of my living room and silently thanked God once again for my new place, even though I had already been there for five months. Caleb had boarded his school bus already and Benjamin was with his father for the remainder of the week, so I had time to marvel at the peace and quiet while I sipped my tea. I continued to think of Adam since the recurring dream from earlier that morning, wondering how in the world his conscience allowed him to stay out of Caleb's life for the past twelve years. I also wondered how I managed to run into people like him—people who abandoned their children who also belonged to families who were able to go on with their lives and pretend their grandchildren/nieces/nephews never existed. It still baffled me that not only was Adam among the worst pieces of shit on this planet, none of his family wanted anything to do with Caleb, *either*. It was the most fucked up twist of bad luck that could have been prevented if I had just...*waited*. Waited to heal from my *fuckedupness* and started and finished school, secured a great career, and *waited* for that one person to find me and love me and marry me. But maybe all this happened so I would have this story to tell, to be able to give a testimony one day...

· · ·

Mateo and I continued to keep things civil, but I knew he was always lurking in the background somewhere, especially when I began realizing there *was* a life outside of being a mother and a student. That's one of the reasons why I began considering moving to a new place—I wanted to leave the past between me and Mateo behind and start all over in a brand new space that he had never stepped foot in, defiling the sanctuary I wanted to create for my children. My decision to prepare myself to move, though, was solidified the day I was reported to Child Protective Services while I was working my shift at the hospital. It was a Sunday when I got the call from a police officer, who was actually calling from my *house* phone. She told me that someone had anonymously called CPS and reported there was a minor left alone in the apartment. She then told me that she couldn't leave Caleb until an adult came to get him.

Fucking SHIT!

The next day, a social worker named Mrs. Jones arrived at the apartment. My face was hot with humiliation as she surveyed my living room, checked out my kitchen and the contents of my fridge, and made sure there was a bed for Caleb to sleep in. The whole time, little Benjamin, who had been almost five months at the time, sat shirtless (the apartment complex had not turned on the air conditioner yet), on my lap and snoozed quietly, while Caleb sat on the leather sofa opposite me, nervously fiddling with his play sword.

After taking a seat next to Caleb, Mrs. Jones asked me if I knew why she was there.

I stared at her for a minute, completely stupefied. She made me feel like a criminal in my own place. I shook my head a little and furrowed my eyebrows. "No, I'm not sure. *Who* reported me?"

She took a breath and looked down at her notes briefly, then looked back up at me. "Well, honestly, I can't say, Ms. Harris. All I can tell you is that the call was placed from a D.C. number."

D.C.? I immediately thought about Mateo, but knew he wanted absolutely nothing to do with the police. Then I thought about his girlfriend Shannon, but didn't know what her motive could be. I relaxed my eyebrows and pulled my lips into a thoughtful scowl. But then again, it could be anyone with a D.C. area code, whether or not they lived in the city. I thought about the neighbor-girl who lived one floor beneath me and how, deep down, I knew I should never trust her. But because I had no proof *not* to, I had given her the benefit of the doubt and probably revealed too much during my stay at Keating House.

"I was at work...and my sister was on her way to come get him, but her car had broken down." That was the truth, actually, *for that weekend* at least. Mrs. Jones didn't need to know that Caleb usually stayed home by himself on weekends and that the Xbox babysat him while I took care of my cancer patients. "It just so happened that I had to work this past Saturday..." I shut my mouth suddenly, my inner self warning me that I'd said enough. I was doing the best I could, but I had no one to keep Caleb on a regular weekend basis. But all that aside, Caleb would be nine-years-old the next week, and Maryland law said that he was able to stay home alone at eight.

Mrs. Jones looked thoughtful. "Well, Ms. Harris, by law, I'm going to have to do background checks on you, talk to your manager...things like that. But from what I see here, you should have nothing to worry about."

I tried to relax, but couldn't believe I was sitting across the room from a fucking *social worker. My God!*

She leaned forward. "To be honest, Ms. Harris, if your son had never answered that front door, I wouldn't even be here today. Do yourself a favor and get him a step-stool so that if anyone knocks, he'll be able to see who's at the door." She gave me a very minute wink of her eye before getting up. "You'll be hearing from me soon."

With that, she left. Caleb continued to fidget with his sword, Benjamin continued to sleep, and I continued to stew in my spot, unable to move as I slowly absorbed everything Mrs. Jones had said to me a few moments before.

I never did hear back from Mrs. Jones, my guess being there

was no investigation begun because there was *nothing to investigate.* And her tipping me off about the footstool almost guaranteed that she was only there because 'by law' she had a job to do. However, almost a year later, I packed up my belongings and moved out of Temple Hills.

• • •

I suddenly became aware of my breathing when my cell phone lit up and began buzzing against the glass of the coffee table. I forced myself back into the present time and set my teacup down next to the phone. Mateo's name showed on the screen, but my heart no longer shimmered at the sight of it. My anxiety, however, kicked in every time he called when he had Benjamin, so I always answered his calls with:

What's wrong? Is Benjamin okay?

Yeah, yeah...he's good. I just called because...because there's something I have to tell you—

—but Benjamin's okay—?

—yeah, Megan. He's fine.

I chuckled in relief. "So you have something to tell me? Hmmm, what did you do *this time,* Mateo?" My question was meant as a joke, but when he paused and took a breath over the phone, I knew what he was about to tell me was serious.

"Man, Megan...some girl is trying to tell me that I'm the father of her kid."

"Huh?" My smile disappeared. "Wait a minute—'some girl'? What happened to Shannon?"

" Megan, you know Shannon left months ago—"

"—ooohhh-yeah, you're right. I forgot." I rubbed my chin and nonchalantly asked, "So, who's the girl?"

"Megan, you don't know her. But I'm telling you because...

because I don't know how this shit happened—"

"—Mateo, you don't know how you got a girl *pregnant*—?"

"No, *Megan*, it wasn't like that..."

"So then, *how* was it, Mateo?" I picked up my teacup and tasted its contents. Still warm enough. I then relaxed against my sofa while Mateo began rambling about this thing and that, and from the speed of his presentation, I knew he was in a race to try to convince me of his bullshit. As I sipped my tea and listened, the only words I was able to pick up were:

It wasn't like that...I used a condom...But it wasn't my condom... Going to have a paternity test done...Maybe she put holes in the damned thing...

"*Holes in the condom*, Mateo?" I sat up and bellowed, almost spilling the sweet liquid from my mouth.

He was angry with my response. "*Megan*! I'm trying to be honest with you..."

Yep, whatever. I cleared my throat, told him I was sorry and that he should continue with his story. I used a napkin to wipe my mouth before downing the rest of my drink. I heard his rambles, but zoned out for the rest of the conversation as I wondered why it was so important for him to explain any of this to me.

• • •

Joshua James was born December 29, 2011, three days after his brother Benjamin was born, three years prior. Mateo never told me his son's birthdate; I just happened to add two and two together when Mateo couldn't "make it to pick up Benjamin for the weekend because [he had] to go to Delaware to do something real quick." And when he called me two days later to inform me that the baby was born and it most definitely belonged to him, two and two finally made four.

"The hospital did a paternity test, and the baby *is actually mine*..."

"Oh! They do paternity tests in hospitals now, Mateo? That quickly?"

"Hold on...hold on...let me call you right back." Click.

I hung up my end, as well, and continued on my brisk walk to my literature class.

• • •

A week after Joshua was born, curiosity took me to the rental row house that *Shannon Bernard* and Mateo had once shared before she decided that she was done with his bullshit. I didn't know exactly what Mateo put that girl through to make her finally end the relationship, but my guess was that he didn't treat her any better than he had treated me. And with the very new baby and Mateo's obvious relationship with the baby's mother, I figured that Shannon finally realized that Mateo would never find contentment with just one woman.

Poor girl. She stayed with Mateo through all the times he kept having babies with *me*...but at least she was smart enough to never get pregnant by him.

Benjamin was already back with his father, spending bonding time with him and his new brother when I arrived. Honestly, I had to give it to Mateo—besides his ongoing drama, he had turned out to be an excellent father, something, for some reason, I had never doubted. Benjamin sat quietly in the bed next to his dad, gently rubbing the baby's curls with his toddler hand as Mateo held his new son in his arms. But not only did I think it was my duty to finally meet Joshua since he *was* my son's little brother, I also wanted to find out why it was *Mateo,* and not the kid's *mother,* who brought the baby home after he was discharged.

"She's just got a lotta shit she's gotta work out, so I had to bring the baby with me."

"Who is 'she,' Mateo?"

"Her name is Mia, Megan."

"Mia. Okay. And where does *Mia* live?"

Mateo took a quiet breath and rolled his eyes. "In Delaware, Megan."

"Oh. Okay." I shut my mouth and swallowed the tinge of jealousy that I felt as I watched Mateo holding a baby he had with another woman whom he obviously loved more than he had ever loved me.

But he never did love you, Megan. That damn conscience of mine. I made a mental note to grab a bottle of wine when I was finished to drown her out for the night.

"You see the new baby, Mommy?"

I swallowed again, and focused on Benjamin. "Yes, I see him, honey. And you're doing an excellent job of taking care of him." I forced myself from my past with Mateo and pushed my envy away because it was the right thing to do. I looked back at Mateo.

"Well, may I please hold him?"

He gave me a quiet smirk, but I could tell he didn't mind; he was just surprised at my request. "Sonny (his nickname for Benjamin), we're going to give the baby to Mommy and let her hold him for a little bit. Then, you can have him back."

"Okay, Daddy!"

Mateo carefully maneuvered himself away from Benjamin and out of the bed as he kept the baby in his arms. I moved closer to the bed and took the baby from him, being overly cautious with his unsteady head. I cradled him in my arms, keeping him close to my chest because he was such a little thing.

I looked back at his father. "Was he premature?"

"A little."

I admired little Joshua James—his skinny baby's body, his loose, black curls, the smooth midnight skin he inherited from his father, and his huge innocent eyes that seemed to immediately trust me as he kept his gaze on me. I fell in love with a child who wasn't even mine.

And it was a good thing, because for the next eight months, Mia stayed away, apparently working some things out on her end, and *I* became Joshua's surrogate mother. It was easy to do; I mean, who wouldn't fall in love with a brand new baby? Anything Mateo needed from me concerning Joshua, I made happen. Caleb and I had even set up Benjamin's old *sleep-n-play* for the times that Joshua came over to sleep. And since Mateo still didn't have his own car, I took him and Joshua to every well-baby check-up.

• • •

"You're crazy," Constance told me one day when she came by the apartment for a drink one evening.

"Yeah, yeah, I know." I handed her a specially-made margarita. "But Mateo doesn't have anyone to help ou—"

"—then he shouldn't keep sticking his dick into other women unprotected!" She took a sip of the doctored up tequila. "Hmmm... this is delicious! Look, I'm just saying, *Megan*"— she motioned towards the *pack-n-play* that was set up in a corner of the living room— "look at this *shit*. You already took care of babies when Caleb and Benjamin were still in diapers. Now you're taking care of *Mateo's* child, out of all people, when he fucked you over so many times."

I took a sip of my own margarita, keeping my eyes on Constance. "It's the right thing to do." She glared back at me and it was all I could do to keep the tasty drink inside my mouth as I muffled my erupting laughter.

• • •

Did I help with baby Joshua because I was in love with Mateo? No, I wasn't anymore. But he had been my security blanket for the past seven years, the one constant I could rely on, whether it was good for me or bad. It had become very easy for me to start imagining a life together with him all over again. One in which it was me, him, and the three boys— Caleb, Benjamin, and Joshua. And that dream seemed even more possible on our trips to the doctor's office for Joshua, and the time Mateo kept Caleb with him and the two boys when a snow storm knocked out my power and I had to go to work...and also, during the occasional nights he'd ask me over for a dinner he'd cook, just for the two of us.

I *still* ached for a family. And the devil knew my soft spots very well.

But Mateo never changed. My apologies—he *did* change because he turned out to be a phenomenal father who did what he had to do for his children. Plus, through the years of parenting Benjamin, he had grown into a kind of "step-father," if you will, for Caleb. But as long as Mateo needed something, he was going to continue using the women in his life. And because he was temporarily laid off again from the Ironworkers since they had run out of work for the season, he needed people in his corner now more than ever.

• • •

I never saw it coming when Mateo called me on a Friday morning to tell me that Mia had reappeared out of thin air and was going to go with him to Joshua's nine-month check-up. And if it was going to be a problem of having her around Benjamin, then he would drop him off to me. And, as always, when he was trying to talk his way out his own bullshit, he spoke quickly:

If it's gonna be a problem, Megan, I can just drop Benjamin off to you—

—*why would it be a problem?* I was a little confused that it wasn't *me* taking him and Joshua to the doctor, but okay...

Because, Megan...look, I'm just saying—

—*saying what, Mateo?*

And then it came. His barrage of words that he talked through swiftly as he tried his best to dress up the cold hard facts that he was trying to tell me, without actually *telling* me. And all I could pick up was:

If it's going to be a problem...he doesn't have to come...I'm going with his mother to the doctor...if you don't want Benjamin around Mia...

Once he was done spilling his story, I took a moment to swallow my tears as I began to fully understand what he was revealing. And even though I wanted to be a vindictive *bitch* and tell him to bring my son back to me because I didn't want him around any other woman, I couldn't. First of all, I had class to get to later that afternoon. And second of all, I knew that I had been dumb as rocks for even getting involved in the first place.

Mia was now back, so Mateo had no use for me anymore past being Benjamin's mother. I was just the stand-in mother, so all family trips to Joshua's primary care and any late-night dinners Mateo had cooked for me prior to Mia's return ceased immediately. A week after Mia showed up for her son's well-baby visit, I took down the *pack-n-play* and returned all blankets, baby toys, and pacifiers to Joshua's father the next time I saw him.

• • •

Looking back, do I have regrets about taking on another woman's child? None at all. Again, little Joshua was very easy to love, and he was also Benjamin's brother. And I couldn't ignore all the times I was able to rely on Mateo to help me with Caleb, even though our relationship had stopped working long before it had even started. I had my own place, my job at the hospital, and I was close to finishing my first degree; it really was all about being able to take care of the kids at that point in my life. Now, would I have done things differently if Mateo had been honest from the start—that he and Mia were actually in a relationship when she had gotten pregnant by him, that he knew it was his baby, and that he needed me for a hot minute to play "Mommy" while his girlfriend got her shit together...?

"I'm not sure," I told Constance before drowning my shot of tequila the same night I had taken down Joshua's make-shift bed.

"Bitch, you're crazy. I would've told Mateo to take that baby back to his mama in Delaware and let *her* deal with him." I watched her take a taste of her drink before giving me a sweet smile. "I am proud of you, though. You helped him out during his time of need. That was very big of you. Even though you *were* dumb as shit."

Our laughs filled the apartment, and I was glad Constance was there to support me.

20

Leash

How do you get away from the person who'll never let you go? Who doesn't want you, but doesn't want to see you make your own happiness *without* them? Who'll treat you like you're less than human, but still have the nerve to be angry when you've decided you've had enough...?

It was now towards the end of August of 2011, and I thought I was *finally* free from the addiction that almost annihilated me over the past eight and a half years, finally finding the guts to walk away from a relationship–a *comfort zone*–that was unsafe for all parties involved, whether or not it would've been just Caleb and me (and sometimes Benjamin) left alone to continuing facing the world on our own.

Mateo and I were long finished. School was getting a bit overwhelming with having both Caleb and Benjamin and my job at the hospital, but I was set to graduate the next spring. And even though I was not in the best apartment or the best neighborhood, I was paying my rent and my bills on time each month, finally handling my business like a *fucking pro*, and I had God to thank for it.

My father even came to visit from Texas that September. On average, we talked at least twice a month, but I hadn't seen him since he had come up for a business trip in D.C., after I had first moved in with Mateo, many moons ago. When he arrived three days ago, he stopped by my apartment and had dinner with me and the boys. That Friday, two days later, he was scheduled to head back home. So the Thursday before, my sister and I had arranged to have lunch with him before he flew back home.

I didn't have to work that day, so I was busy getting myself ready to meet him at Avery's apartment, where he had been staying. Caleb was at school and Benjamin was in his Pre-K class. As I got ready to apply foundation to my face, I heard a knock at the door.

I looked through the peephole, making sure it was Mateo. Not that I was expecting him, but who else could be at my door at ten in the morning, uninvited? Opening it, I saw that he had little Joshua in his arms, and I invited them inside.

"Hey, come in. What's up?" I had to leave soon, so I was hoping that whatever brought Mateo to my house unexpectedly would soon be resolved so I could finish getting dressed.

"What's up?" He put Joshua's diaper bag by the front door of the apartment. "Do you mind if I give Joshua a bath real quick? I have no hot water in the house."

I sighed, almost to myself. "Sure, go 'head. But I gotta hurry up and get outta here."

He looked at me and peered into my face as if to search for something that I was trying to keep hidden. "Really? Where are *you* going?"

I thought about my answer for a second. I didn't want him to know I was going to meet my father because I knew he'd be jealous that I finally had a life outside of him.

"I need to go to the bank real quick," I answered. I looked down at my watch. "Here, let me take him from you so you can run his bath."

Mateo carefully handed the baby to me as he continued to watch me. He smirked. "Yeah, right. The *bank*?"

I took the baby and said nothing.

"Well, I gotta use the bathroom real quick, so hold him for me, please."

I watched Mateo make his way through my apartment and into the bathroom. He still kept his shoes on, never ever respecting my wishes to leave his shoes by the door. I didn't say anything this time because I had things to do. I carried Joshua into the bedroom, laid his now chubby body onto the bed, and began removing his clothes. His small, black face, framed by the thick, curly hair beamed up at me. And my heart melted.

Ten minutes later, Mateo was still in the bathroom. "Damn," I whispered to myself, as I watched Joshua try to figure out how to get down from the bed. I picked him up before he hurt himself, his long fingernails accidentally swiping the side of my face. I put him back on the bed and examined his hands. "Joshua, you're gonna need your nails cut, buddy." It wasn't uncommon for me to cut his nails whenever I saw that they needed to be cut, during the times he'd been at my place. I left him on the bed and fetched my fingernail clippers.

I held the little one in my lap and steadied his miniature black hands inside my own and began clipping carefully. Upon the start of the third fingernail, I heard Mateo flush the toilet, run some water, and then turn it off. He stuck his head outside the door and looked at me.

"What are you doing?" He asked as if he were accusing me of something terrible.

I stopped. "I'm cutting his nails. They're too long."

"No, *Megan*. I have to go. I don't have time for that right now."

I put the clippers down. "Um, okay. Fine." I kept holding onto Joshua as Mateo popped his head back into the bathroom. I heard the bathtub water running and figured he was running a bath for Joshua finally, until I heard him start the shower. I wondered what the hell he was doing when he knew I had to go. I thought he only came to give his *son* a bath.

I shrugged my shoulders and picked up my clippers, figuring that he *did*, in fact, have time for me to cut the boy's nails, if he was now showering.

Almost ten minutes later, I was down to Joshua's last nail, and Mateo had turned off the shower water. He poked his head back out of the bathroom and looked at me with disdain. "Megan! I told you not to cut the boy's nails!"

I stopped immediately and inadvertently dropped the clippers, feeling that same accusatory tone once again, as if he suddenly didn't want me around his son anymore. I was hurt, not understanding what the problem was because whenever Joshua had been with me, I did everything from feed him to change his dirty diapers. And what was the father doing at my place again…?? Using *my* water in *my* apartment to bathe *his* child…and bold enough to tell *me* what to do and not to do.

Then it came to me. Mateo probably didn't want Mia to know that another woman was cutting her baby's nails—*sneaky dickhead*—but he and I were *done*, so who cared? As far as I was concerned, they *both* needed to grow up.

I put the innocent baby back onto the bed and made my way out to the dining room table to avoid the fight that Mateo was trying to pick. I said nothing because I knew where this was headed. I just wanted to get the rest of my make-up and clothes on and meet my father and sister. I sat down on one of the wooden chairs at the dining room table and took a breath. I would wait there until

Mateo bathed Joshua and got the hell out of my place.

But he followed me. And here is where I ask the question again: how do you get away from the one person who won't *let* you get away? Not two seconds after I sat down, Mateo was behind me, breathing his fire down my neck. "Megan, I fucking told you *not* to cut that boy's nails. He has a mother—let *her* do it. How would *you* feel if some other bitch cut *our* son's hair?"

'He has a mother'... and yet, Mateo brought the baby to *me*. Enough of this. I stood slowly and faced him. "Sure, Mateo, I get it. But just to make sure I'm clear next time, is there anything *else* you would like to add to the *do-not-do-to-Joshua* list?"

He smacked the right side of my face, knocking me to the floor.

"You fucking bastard!" I yelled as hard as I could, kicking his left knee with as much force as I could gather while covering the burn to my face.

But I could never hurt Mateo. Cursing him, yelling at him, and returning his blows only made him dangerously angrier. Before I knew it, he was bent to my level and had his big black hands around my throat, choking the life out of me.

"*Bitch*, what did you say to me?"

I screamed and cried inside of my head, not able to do it out loud because he had my throat clamped shut. All of this was because he realized that my world no longer revolved around him, even *after* he made a kid with somebody else.

I attempted to shut my eyes, not wanting to look at the evil that flowed freely from Mateo, but I couldn't even do that. With the grip he had around my neck, my eyes felt as if they were being ejected from my face. When I finally found the strength to raise my arms and claw at his hands, he finally let me go. I gasped and choked up a little mucus. With sweat pouring from his black head and the rapid rise and fall of his chest, he let his arms drop and relax next to his sides, visibly spent. That's when I thought I caught a glimpse of humanity replacing the darkness covering his face, and not wanting to wait a second longer, I scrambled to my feet and tried to bolt for the front door.

But he regained his bearings at the speed of light and grabbed me by my neck again and pinned me to the bare wall of the dining area. I buried my nails into his skin once more as I tried to break free from his grasp. He let me go again. I started running towards the only bedroom in the tiny apartment, screaming for my life as I prayed that one of my neighbors would hear me and call the police. When I made it to the room, I scurried inside the tight space of the walk-in closet and crouched down next to some shoe boxes. Clutching my knees to my chest, I prayed that Mateo would find his sanity the moment that I was out of his sight, and decide to take his son and just *leave*.

But he followed me into the closet. *Damn it!* I couldn't even get to my cell to call the police because the damn phone was somewhere in the kitchen!

He closed the door and now, I was his prisoner. In my own home, the home I had turned into a sanctuary for my boys. He slowly took a seat in front of me, like I was his fucking child, and began talking...nice and slow. Sweat continued to drip from his once-handsome head as his quick *huffs* and *puffs* began to lessen. He proceeded to talk about nothing that made sense to me:

Don't you know I loved you...? Why don't you ever listen...? Why do you want to be both man and woman...? Where were you going anyway...? To the bank...? Yeah, right...That boy has a mother... You NEVER listen... You bring this shit onto yourself... Baby, I'm sorry... Megan, do you hear me...? Etcetera, etcetera...

I tuned him out, sobbing as I silently asked myself why this shit kept happening, especially since *we were no longer together*!

"...do you understand what I'm saying to you, *Megan*!"

I blinked my eyes back to the present terror. No, I didn't understand him, and I didn't care to. "Fuck *you*," I sneered through my sniffles.

He hit me square in the face again, knocking me from my crouched position. I fell backwards into the shoe boxes. I cried out in surprise, cradling my face once again where his hand had landed, and kept my eyes on him. However, his pupils began to soften as he wiped the sweat from his brow and reached his hand out to me. "Megan...Megan. I'm sorry."

I continued to hold my face and watch him as I tried to understand his rationale. Suddenly becoming aware of the gentle splatters of spring rain against the bedroom windows, I vowed to never let Mateo cross my home's threshold again. I gave him my hand. He helped me up. The minute he turned his back, though, I made another attempt for the front door. I made it all the way back to my exit, and was even able to reach for my sneakers...

...and then he gave a quick yank of the leash he had kept around my neck for the past eight years, once more.

He cornered me, placing himself between me and the safety of the door. "Where the fuck are you going, *MEGAN*???"

Jesus, I couldn't stand the way he pronounced my name. I couldn't help myself. "Leave me the fuck alone, *Mateo*! Stay here for as long as you want—I don't care—just let me get out of here, *please*!" The vein inside the top of his forehead, that infamous vessel that had been a steady part of our relationship, began pulsating, indicating that the demon was soon to escape again. Before I knew it, Mateo was back to wrapping his hand around my throat before effortlessly flinging me to the sofa that was by the door, like I was a bag of trash.

He choked me while looking me dead in the eyes. *"This is why we can't be together, Megan. Because you make me do shit like this!"*

WHAT!!! I screamed inside my head again while trying to catch any breath I could while his hands remained clutched to my throat. That egotistical *asshole* still thought he was God's gift to me!

After ten more seconds of being forced to watch his wicked glare, he let go of my leash. Wiping his sweaty brow for the third time that morning, he traveled back to the only bathroom in the apartment, leaving me by the front door. I wiped my own face, trying to rid it of the mixture of sweat and spit and hatred that he had sprayed on me throughout the course of that hour. After hearing the sound of water starting from the faucet, I darted out of the apartment as fast as I could without even wasting time putting my tennis shoes on. With bare feet, I ran as fast as they could carry me through the puddled parking lot and towards my car.

I raced towards Constance's apartment complex, ignoring the 40 mph speed limit. Five miles later, I was beating down the door to her apartment with panicked fists.

It didn't take her long to open the door. "Oh, my God, Megan... What the *hell*...??"

Huffing and puffing, I rushed past her. "Huffing and puffing, I rushed past her. "I'm sorry...he hurt me...and I didn't know where else to go..." *Huff, huff.* I stopped for a minute to allow my breaths to catch up with my speech. "I don't even have my phone on me... or else, I would've called first." *Huff, huff.* I leaned my body over towards her floor and tried to steady my breathing.

"Or your shoes..."

I straightened my body. "My *what?*"

"Your *shoes*, Megan." She walked over and looked at my wet feet. "What the fuck happened to your shoes?"

I sighed deeply. "They're at the fucking house, Constance. I had to hurry the hell outta there before he tried to hit me again. I didn't have time for my shoes."

"Oh, my God." Constance met my eyes. "Megan, what did he *do* to your face??"

"My face?" I put my hands up and gingerly felt around, now realizing the pain. I opened my mouth to explain, but now *that* was beginning to hurt, too.

Just then, she opened her mouth wide and put both her light brown hands to her face. "Megan...your eye is fucking swelling. Here, come to the bathroom."

She offered her hand and I took it as she led me down the slender hallway to her bathroom. She flicked on the light and I instantly blinked twice as the sudden flash of brightness burned my eyes.

"Look at your face."

I did as I was told, gasping at my reflection. I had been in the middle of applying make-up when Mateo made his surprise visit, so there was nothing but black smudges of mascara and eyeliner shading the bottoms of my eyes. I didn't remember being struck in my mouth, but there was a thick bloody fissure splitting my bottom lip. The right side of my face was swelling quickly where Mateo had kept bringing down his heavy hand. My hair had been yanked from its former bun and was now resembling the wildness of a lion's mane. But the worst part of it all was the numerous red and purple marks that intermingled with the scratches and spots of blood around my neck from where Mateo had choked me several times. I carefully looked to my left at Constance and began to cry"

"Oh, my God. What did I do, Constance? What did I *do* to deserve this?"

She watched me cry for a second, sympathetic tears starting to form in her own eyes. I abhorred breaking down in front of others because it exposed my vulnerability, my weakness, my stupidity. Eight long years, and I was still going through this same shit, all because I just had to open my door.

"Hold on," Constance told me quietly. I watched her through burning, pitiful eyes as she left her bathroom. Then I looked back at my ugly reflection in the mirror. I shook my head slowly, feeling regretful.

Constance returned a minute later with her house phone. She handed it over to me. "You have to call the police, Megan."

I turned from the mirror and faced my friend. "Nooo, you know I can't do that, Constance."

She spoke to me softly, but sternly. "Megan, you *have* to." She motioned towards the mirror. "Look at what he did to you! It's not right! What if Caleb and Benjamin had been there to see all this...?"

But Mateo had made sure they weren't there. Caleb was in school, and Benjamin was in his pre-K class in D.C. And even though little Joshua had been there, he didn't count: he was too little to talk or do anything while I was getting thrown around. Mateo made sure he got me when I was all alone

I reluctantly took the phone, not wanting to do what I knew I had to. I never had the courage before to make him pay for the hurt he caused me. I just kept thinking that if I got away from him then all of the abuse would stop. And it *had* stopped shortly after I had Benjamin and banned him from my apartment back *then*. It had been almost three whole years since the last time he and I had gotten into it.

"Megan. What was he *even doing in your house?*"

I shook my head slowly, feeling ashamed, and not wanting to go through this right now. "Long story short, he needed my bathtub to wash Joshua. That was it. I was actually on my way out to

222

meet my father."

"Oh, damn." Suddenly, she raised her eyebrows. "Megan, is he still gonna pick Benjamin up from school?"

"I don't know, Constance. That's the last thing I'm thinking about right now." I took a deep breath and looked down at my watch. Benjamin didn't get out of pre-K for another couple of hours, and I didn't see any reason why his father wouldn't be able to get him.

"I need to call my dad..."

Constance tipped her head towards her phone. "But first, you need to call the police."

I sighed again. "And if he goes to jail, then what the hell am I gonna do about Benjamin and school and my job? Who's gonna take Benjamin to and from D.C. for school?

"Make the call, Megan . I'll help you—"

I scoffed at her. "And how in the hell will you do *that*? The boy goes to school every day, in *D.C.*—how will you be able to help me with that?" Constance knew me well, and she understood I wasn't trying to insult her in any way. I was *just so frustrated* and I hated when people offered to help but really never meant it, having learned long ago not to depend on anyone who had no legal responsibility to me or my children.

She sighed, becoming frustrated with *my* frustration. "You're right—I wouldn't be able to get him to and from school. But there is a different way. And you're not gonna stand here and tell me that you're gonna let him get away with this shit one more time, just because you don't know yet 'what [you're] gonna do with Benjamin.' I already told you that I would help, but right now, Megan, you need to call the police. *Now*."

I blew out another puff of air, feeling my anxiety start to beat wildly against my chest wall once again before making its way to my head, which was starting to pound. I stared at Constance while she returned the stare, both of us locked in a standoff as she continued to hold her phone out to me. She was right. I reluctantly took the black phone from her and pressed the ON button and dialed the non-emergency number for the police.

• • •

When I made it back to my apartment two hours later, it was vacated and unlocked. Mateo and his son were gone. I had to hurry and clean the mess that was made while Mateo was kicking me around earlier before Caleb made it home from school. I didn't visit with my father on his last day in town because I couldn't let him see my blue and purple face. After making sure everything was back in its place, I slathered more make-up onto my face and throat and donned a hoodie so that Caleb would be none the wiser.

• • •

On January 27, 2012, I downed two Valiums with a shot of Smirnoff before appearing as a witness for the state of Maryland. Even though Mateo told the judge that he was sorry for what he did to me, the judge told him:

That's great and everything, um, Mr. James, but what's going to happen the next time you hurt her and you wind up killing her—are you going to say you're sorry then?

False imprisonment, second degree assault, and trespassing. Mateo was then sentenced to 180 days in the Upper Marlboro Correctional Facility.

After the judge handed over his sentence, I watched in quiet horror as the bailiff swiftly approached Mateo from behind and handcuffed him, almost as if the bailiff had already known that

Mateo was going to jail. Mateo was then led towards my left to the exit of the courtroom, next to the judge's chair. It would be close to four months when I would see him again.

After leaving the courthouse, I made my way into D.C. to withdraw Benjamin from school. The school secretary gave me a hard time about it because she insisted that both parents needed to be present since *both parents* had enrolled him. I was impatient, tapping my fingers against the desk that separated me and her. I now absolutely loathed being in D.C., or anywhere that was remotely *close* to Mateo's house. I was already feeling guilty that I had to take my son away from his friends and his amazing teachers, and I just wanted to hurry up and get the shit over and done with before I burst into tears.

"Listen. I'm sorry, but my son's father is not here, and he won't be here for a long time—he went to jail just an hour ago. So, can I please just withdraw my son? I have no other choice."

She looked at me for a long second before granting my wish. If she had given me anymore trouble, then I would've signed my son out for an early dismissal and that would have been the last day the school would see him. Simple as that. It was only pre-k, for Chrissakes!

And to make matters worse, I felt like shit on Benjamin's last day at school. His teacher had made a beautiful card for him, complete with his picture in the middle of the purple construction paper, and signatures from all his other classmates surrounding it. I almost cried when she handed it to Benjamin and wished me good luck. *Damn it!* Why did all this have to happen?

I had to change my work schedule to Saturdays, Sundays, and Tuesdays. Benjamin would stay with Caleb during the weekends, and before I went to work on Saturdays, I had to make sure that there were enough snacks and cooked meals to last the boys throughout the weekend. Every hour, on the hour, I would call from work to make sure the kids were okay. I have to give it to Caleb—even though it wasn't fair that he had to become the instant "nanny" for Benjamin, he turned into an astounding big brother.

On the Tuesdays that I worked, I would get up at 4:45 in the morning, get ready for my shift, and carry the sleeping Benjamin to the car so I could drop him off to Constance's house by 6 a.m. Most of the time, he would already be dressed in his daytime clothes by the time I put him to sleep Monday nights so I wouldn't have to worry about that come Tuesday morning. After dropping him off at Constance's, I would make the 35-minute drive to work.

I was scheduled to graduate with my Associate's that May, but I still had one more online class to take, and one inside the actual classroom on Mondays. So on Monday mornings, I would get Benjamin together, drop him off at Constance's for two hours, then come back for him after class. Some Mondays, she would even offer to keep him for the rest of the day and overnight since I had to work the next day.

Thank God Caleb took the bus to and from school, and he was old enough to stay home with his brother. No, I'm lying—he probably *wasn't* allowed at nearly thirteen-years-old to keep little Benjamin all day long, but I had no other choice.

In late February, I received a call from Mia, Joshua's mother. I was shocked, considering she had remained a ghost to me from the time her son was born, but I asked her very nicely what she needed.

"Well, I wanted to know if I could pick Benjamin up someday for the weekend, so he can see Joshua..."

Hmmm. From what I knew, this woman couldn't even keep her own kid, and now she wanted to pick my own up for the weekend...?

"Um, I'll have to talk to Mateo about this because I don't remember his mentioning any of this to me."

After I politely declined, I received a phone call from the correctional facility twenty minutes later.

Will you accept the charges from a Mr. Mateo James?

Sure.

Megan! What the fuck do you mean, Mia can't go pick up Benjamin? I want my sons to see each other. It's not their fault that I'm here…!

And it's not my fault, either!

I angrily clicked my OFF button and immediately changed my phone number. So all the times I had been helping out with Joshua, what the hell was *she* doing?? And to ask if she could get Benjamin, completely out of the blue…? Was she out of her *fucking* mind? Was *he* out of his fucking mind? I didn't know who the hell she was. I didn't know her last name, where she lived, where she worked, what she even *looked* like. All I knew was that I had served as the proxy mother for almost a year, because according to her shitty-ass baby's father, she wasn't able to take care of her child at the time.

And *now* she was? Along with *my* kid, too? Yeah, okay.

I didn't give Mateo my new number. I wrote him a letter and let him know that if he wanted to contact his son while he was away, he could just write to him, and I would read the letters to him.

I walked away and never looked back.

21

Darjeeling

"Megan...did you hear me?"

I blinked, suddenly remembering my current location before my mind had decided to disconnect and travel to the nether regions of the universe, and turned my eyes back to Adam. Inside the cozy comfort of Lola's Coffee Shop, only a modest mahogany table separated the two of us where time and space had once occupied. It was nearing 8:45 on a quiet Saturday morning, and the only customer inside was a young woman who sat by the glass-door entrance, her head buried inside a laptop.

"I'm sorry...what were you saying?" The cream-colored armchair that provided rest for my bottom was soft and inviting, but I couldn't relax as I fought hard to wrap my head around the fact that I was now within the same breathing space of the man who had been able to successfully disappear from our son's entire childhood. I shifted my weight a little and inspected my pale-yellow sundress, smoothing out an invisible wrinkle over my knee. I looked back up, surprised to meet a pair of light brown eyes that were etched with a familiar concern...and a certain kind of intimidation that I wasn't used to seeing. Adam opened his mouth to reply, but the barista beat him to it.

"Order up for Megan and Adam!"

We quickly took our eyes from one another and stood at the same time. "Don't worry, I got it," Adam told me quietly. But he hadn't gotten me much of anything in almost two decades or so, so I certainly didn't need him to start doing it then.

"No, I can get it—"

But he held his sandy brown hand out across the wooden table in gentle objection and told me, "Megan, I got it."

• • •

"You may not believe me, but I never meant to hurt you, Megan. I never meant to stay away from Caleb for so long..."

I was hearing Adam, but the warmth of the Darjeeling tea that I held carefully between my hands had me mesmerized. A black tea that gets its name from the Darjeeling district in India in which it's grown, it had become my usual order at Lola's whenever Adam and I were able to steal early mornings together over a lifetime ago. He had been the one to introduce me to it when I was eighteen—four years younger than he'd been—and I had valued his guidance because I trusted him with my whole heart and soul. Bringing the huge ceramic teacup to my lips, I carefully sampled the tea's temperature, but it was too hot to drink. I placed it back down onto the table and looked at Adam. Hunching my shoulders, I mustered the only response I could come up with:

I don't know if it's even for me to believe at this point. Caleb is twenty-one now—shouldn't you be having this conversation with him?

I laid my hands on the table and folded them in front of me, pursing my lips for a second as another thought came to me. "Better yet, since he's now an adult, you really don't even need me here with you right now; you could've just emailed me for his contact information"

I watched him blink a few times, his surprise at my unexpected curtness showing on his still handsome face. He opened his mouth to say something but decided to close it back. With a quiet, almost defeated sigh, he picked up his latte and took a sip. Then he looked back at me with those same eyes I had fallen in love with once upon a time and humbly said:

"I didn't know how to get into contact with him—"

"—and *yet*, you were able to figure out how to get into contact with *me*?" I heard myself blurt out the question as I reflexively leaned over the round table, coming within inches of Adam's face. My voice wasn't raised; however, I momentarily looked up from our place to see if anyone else in the shop had seen my reaction. But other than the two baristas at the coffee bar, the woman with the computer, and now an elderly husband and wife couple who were perusing the pastry section, there was no one else inside Lola's other than an elderly husband and wife couple who were perusing the pastry section. I swallowed thickly, disappointed in myself that nearly eighteen years later, this man, who had incredibly remained an enigma for all of Caleb's life, was still able to rouse the anger and hurt that I believed had been buried very deep inside of me until the end of time. In all honesty, though, throughout the passing years, I had only merely learned how to accept what I couldn't change, finally understanding that I needed to move on as I lied to myself over and over again that I'd forgiven and forgotten, and that Adam's incredible sin meant absolutely nothing to me anymore.

"Your social media," he answered, still keeping his voice even and calm. I continued to observe him as he closed his mouth and swallowed...as I continued to hold my body erect. He cautiously removed his eyes from my stare and reached for his latte. He took another drink, and when he placed the cup back down, he began to fidget with it before returning his attention to me.

"I've been keeping up with you—and Caleb—for all these years. I saw some pictures of Caleb from the time he was in middle school, I think, to the last one you had posted from his graduation from Fort Benning last year. I followed a couple of links and got your website...and then I found your contact information. I've had your email for a while...but I really wasn't sure if I should even approach you."

I kept my eyes on him, but allowed my body to relax. Suddenly, I remembered my tea. I relaxed my posture and let my eyes drop. Gathering the teacup back into my hands, I was grateful for the warmth that seemed to instantly temper my hostility. I held it up to my lips and carefully tasted it once again. The temperature was still hot, but it was just the way I liked it. As I took another sip, its floral scents playfully floated towards my nose, beckoning me back to the far away past, a past that I had decided to let go of when Caleb had his second birthday and I had realized that Adam wanted nothing more to do with us. His number had changed, his email address had been deactivated, and he had even gone AWOL from the military. I took a few more swallows of the translucent goodness, a taste I had also made sure to forget since I had last stepped inside the cafe with Adam, almost 18 years ago to the day, the very last time he had seen me and Caleb. I sunk back into my arm chair and crossed a bare leg over the other, keeping the teacup close to my heart, as I savored the aroma of the spicy tea, which I had denied myself all these years in order to forget Adam ever existed so that I could move on and be a good mother to Caleb.

"Megan, I had to come here first to tell you, from the bottom of my heart, that I'm sorry."

I glanced at him and gave a slight nod of my head, placing my attention back onto my teacup. I took another taste of the fragrant flavor and turned my head to the right as my mind drifted to happier times, when I was a bubbly eighteen-year-old girl who had fallen in love for the very first time, and would've done anything and everything to hold onto that feeling for longer than I was able to.

"Megan..."

I peered at him through my left peripheral but I was unable to respond. Fresh tears from a dam that had been built so many years ago were now breaking through, getting caught inside of my tightened throat. I drank some more of the Darjeeling and tried to hold onto those memories, but as the warmth of the tea began to fade, the spice of the liquid started to give way to the slightly musky undertones that are common to it, and those sweet remembrances took me to my first day at the home for unwed mothers...to the hundreds of times that I had to wait until 7 p.m. to use the group telephone so that I could call Adam at the Coast Guard Station, Annapolis to give him updates on a pregnancy he cared nothing for...

"Megan...?"

I wiped at my eye and sat up straight once more, placing the remainder of the Darjeeling on the table that separated Adam and me. The floral scents were now gone, and suddenly I remembered why I had stopped drinking the tea in the first place. I looked at the biological father of my son. His arm was stretched across the table, as if he would try to reach out to me, if I let him. But I didn't. I fished a ball point pen out of my handbag and quickly scribbled Caleb's cell number onto the paper napkin provided by Lola's and left Adam and the Darjeeling for—

—*beep, beep, beep, beep!*

The sudden beeping interrupted my plans for a dramatic exit and I raised my head to search for the intrusive noise. My eyes darted to and fro to uncover the source, but the only thing I could see was a suddenly empty Lola's. The girl with the laptop was gone, the elderly couple was nowhere to be found...even the baristas were missing from their positions behind the glass counter and espresso machines. When I focused back onto Adam, his expression of regret began to melt into the color of his eyes and skin, and soon the red of his t-shirt along with the denim of his blue jeans followed suit, finally dissipating into a body of powdery purple that I could no longer make out. I began to panic as the rest of Lola's became a blur and I felt my throat begin to close.

Beep, beep, beep...!

I closed my eyes and covered my ears and turned my head to the left, where the sound was the strongest. Suddenly, Lola's was completely black and I found myself reopening my eyes–

—*beep, beep, beep*!

I rubbed my eyes and forced myself to make some sense of my surroundings. When I heard the fourth succession of *beeps!* I saw the inside of my bedroom and slowly began to understand that I had only been dreaming. Using the back of my hand, I wiped at my wet eyes and reached over the left side of the bed for my cell, which must've fallen to the floor during my sleep, and dismissed the alarm.

I never dreamed of Adam Hartley again

Afterword

Mateo was bitter with me after being released from jail 60 days after his initial 90-day sentence. Our "relationship" was a bit of a struggle for quite some time; he had even enlisted his cousin (yes, the same cousin who had drained my scant bank account years before) to serve me papers for child support and full custody of Benjamin. There was so much drama between Mateo and me that ensued during this time, mostly because Mia was absolutely convinced that I wanted her boyfriend back. I can assure you, that was *not* the case, as I was engaged to get married in another year, and could care less about their shit.

Two days before our day in family court, Mateo called to see if I would reconsider.

"Megan, can we work something out?"

"We already *had* something worked out before you sued me for custody, Mateo."

"But do you really want a judge to decide what happens to our *son*?"

"*You* took me to court, Mateo, and *I* took the day off for it. So yes, if that's what has to happen, then *that's* what has to happen." Mateo's need for control was still inside of him, and I realized that even though he didn't have access to me anymore, he still had Benjamin to use as a pawn. As long as he still had the power to piss me off, he would keep that control over me. So, one day I woke up and just stopped caring. Arrived at the conclusion that I had to so I could continue moving away from Mateo James. Had to come to the realization that God had tried to warn me before, with the deaths of Isaiah and Junior, to stop seeing Mateo, but I never listened. Now *this* was the bed I had made and I needed to understand that I had no power to make this situation better, that it wasn't going to be perfect or be what I wanted it to be, and I should've known this from day *one*.

Turned out, the judge gave us joint custody. He had even put in writing which days Mateo had Benjamin, and which days *I* had him. Even deal.

Once I took my feelings away– whether they were good or bad– I took Mateo's power away.

My relationship with Veronica remained the same. She didn't attend my graduation for my associate's, and she didn't attend commencement for my bachelor's. She didn't see me get married, and after Caleb, the other grandchildren hardly know her. Maybe I should've stopped caring long ago, but I had yet to grow from the little girl who ached terribly for her mother's approval. At thirty-two years of age, I was still finding validation in what other people thought of me.

Nevertheless, it was during my sister's passing when I finally realized that I had to stop taking on my mother's dysfunction as my own...as if it were *me* and not *her*, or even a combination of the both of us. Or, as if the miserable relationship we had with one another was just a consequence of a fucked up childhood *she* may have had.

But she had loved my sister *Avery*, proving her capacity to love her children—she just wasn't able to love *me*. I'm not sure what happened, or exactly *when* it happened, but somewhere during the period of my early childhood and the time I transitioned into my preteen years, *something* occurred between us that set into motion the repugnance she felt for me for all of my years. And for the life of me, I was never able to figure it out.

But what difference did it still make when I was now forty-years-old and Caleb had made it to twenty-one? I was all for forgetting the past, accepting Veronica and me for the defection that we had always been. But when Avery's wife called me on Christmas night of 2020, the day before Benjamin's thirteenth birthday, to tell me that Avery had just choked on her dinner, lost consciousness and went into cardiac arrest, I would soon understand just how much my mother wished it had been *me* who wound up on life support, instead of her very precious, youngest daughter.

Avery's spirit had already departed by the time her body was rushed to the emergency room, two nights before I had snuck in to see her. And I say *snuck in* because what Olivia had originally told me was that there were *zero visitors allowed*, which was strange to me given that my sister was just waiting to be declared brain dead. As we were in the middle of the Coronavirus pandemic at the time, however, what she said didn't sound too far-fetched. But, *I* worked in the hospital and knew that even with the Coronavirus restrictions in place, immediate family members did still have the right to say goodbye to their loved ones.

It was that Monday morning, two days after Avery had been admitted when Olivia called me with a sudden change to the visiting hours. Now, *two visitors* in total could visit...and they had to come at the same time, on the same day...and stay for no more than 20 minutes.

Really...?

"I feel like I've already said my goodbyes, so I'm willing to give my spot up to you and your mother if she wants to go."

"Thanks Olivia." I ended the call and texted my mother. But she let me know that she would not be in attendance...that she couldn't see her *baby* like that...that she wouldn't believe Avery was dead until she *comes to [her] to say she's gone.*

She'll be cremated and then the ashes will be split between me and Olivia.

That was the next text from Veronica. Strange– Avery still had me and our father that her ashes could have been split among, along with her niece and four nephews. And how was the cremation already decided...?

I texted Veronica again. "Mom, Avery told you she wanted to be cremated?"

"Yes."

All of this was crazy to me, considering that as far as I knew, Avery's trip to the hospital this last time was a complete surprise. Now, suddenly, Olivia and my mother were already aware of her last wishes...?

I texted my father next, informing him of the amended visiting hours, without giving much thought to the fact that Olivia had failed to mention if she had invited my father or not to come to the hospital. But I gave him the visitor information, anyway, and let Olivia know that he'd be catching the next flight from Texas. However, it would be four hours later when she finally texted me:

That's fine, but your mother can NEVER know about this.

Okay. So Avery is on a vent, and the most important thing to my mother and Olivia is making sure that *Dad* does not show up, out of all fucking things to focus on?? I was very aware that Veronica still harbored the hatred she felt for my father since their divorce some thirty years before. But in no way did I ever expect she'd exercise that anger up until the *very end* of my sister's life by making sure he didn't get to see his youngest daughter for the last time.

I texted back *Okay* and said nothing else. But when I got home that Monday evening, something told me to call the hospital to clarify the *actual* visiting policy.

"No, any immediate family member can come between today and Wednesday when we finally perform the tests to look at her brain function. And you can stay for 15 minutes." This rule, I would find out later, was per *Olivia*.

That was Avery's nurse, Amy. I perked up. "So I can come now?"

"Yes, that will be fine—"

"—well, I'm almost two hours away and won't get there until about 9:30; will *that* be okay?"

"Yes, that's fine. I won't be here since they'll be changing shifts soon, but I'll let her next nurse know that you'll be arriving sometime this evening."

"Thanks a lot. I appreciate it." I got off the phone with nurse Amy, downed a valium, packed a couple of energy drinks, and made the two-hour drive into Delaware.

Avery's swollen body was infused with numerous lines for feeding, urinating, and IV hydration. The clear tube that emerged from her mouth was connected to the ventilator that constantly pumped air into her failed lungs. She was already gone before she was actually *gone*, and for a second, I wondered if she were standing right there next to me as we both watched her peaceful body...

"If you have any questions, please feel free to ask."

I spun around towards the entrance of my sister's room and met her nurse. "Hi, I'm her sister. Thank you so much..."

"Hi. I'm Linda, your sister's nurse–"

"—and I'm Megan."

"Nice to meet you. And again, I'm here, so if you have any questions, please feel free to ask."

"Thank you. But all of this because she choked on her food?"

Linda shook her head somberly. "Yes. From the original report, she had somehow started choking and was never able to clear her airway. Her... *partner...*?"

I nodded. "Yes, her wife Olivia..."

Linda nodded again. "Yes, thank you. Her wife tried the Heimlich but was unsuccessful. So she tried to perform CPR when your sister lost consciousness. She then went into cardiac arrest, and by the time the paramedics arrived to restart her heart, her brain had lost too much oxygen."

I nodded again, with no words for the few quiet seconds that nurse Linda and I stood next to Avery.

But things still weren't adding up for me. "But she was confused just before this happened and was in the hospital for pneumonia a week ago..."

"Oh, really...?"

"Yes." I wanted to continue talking but Linda's sudden change in tone told me that she was at liberty to reveal only what she had just disclosed, as per Olivia, I was sure. How could she *not* know that Avery was just hospitalized for pneumonia and altered mental status just 10 days before? Even if Avery hadn't been in that same hospital, her medical record had to have followed her.

I nodded my head in understanding and told Linda *thank you*, turning back to my sister, aware that that quarter of an hour I was allotted would be my last time with her. I waited until I heard the somber sound of Linda's hospital clogs fade away as she left Avery's room. I then let my sister know that Caleb, Benjamin, the three youngest children– Savannah, Cody, and Matthew– and my husband said goodbye and that they were sorry they couldn't come to the hospital. I was so angry with Olivia and my mother for trying to cut everyone else out of Avery's last days on Earth. I was *so angry*. I was reminded of the time of my grandmother's passing, which happened in Virginia. Yes, along with Veronica, her whole side of the family had excommunicated me when I got pregnant with Caleb. But even in my grandmother's last few years, I was there to help my mother help *her* mother through her debilitating dementia, whenever she had been in town. And yet, I was *still* not invited to the funeral. I will always remain an embarrassment to Veronica.

I continued standing there, thinking about my sister's condition prior to this dreadful day, trying to make *some kind of sense* out of all this. I *knew* Avery was sick from the time I was told she was fighting the doctors off when she had been admitted the last time, less than two weeks before, to the time she was discharged but still so confused that she attempted to trade her car in, during a snowstorm. She had only succeeded in slipping on her and Oliva's icy driveway and breaking her ankle in the process. Soon after her ankle cast was set, we talked on the phone and I heard the confusion in her child-like voice. But every time I asked her (when she was coherent) and Olivia what the MRI and CT scan results were concluding, I was always told they showed nothing.

But she was 38 and confused, and went into cardiac arrest and brain death from a *fucking hot dog*...?

My eyes remained glued to Avery. It did strike me as odd that Olivia had omitted the name of the hospital Avery had been taken to, as well as her room number, but I figured that maybe in her state of panic, she had just forgotten to tell me. But when I had offered to drive to Delaware to be Olivia's support system, as well as get physically closer to Avery in case I was able to visit, I was told

241

not to worry about it...that Olivia's *sister* was on her way to their mobile home in the city of Dover.

I thought back to the Thursday before the weekend I was to graduate. It had been six years since I last saw Veronica, and Avery and Olivia were picking her up from BWI Airport and bringing her to my house for an impromptu gathering before we all met again in New Hampshire. I was almost excited that my mother was going to witness me graduate–*finally!* – but understood she came to see it with her own eyes, and to find some kind of peace in doing what she was supposed to do as a mother (or maybe Avery had begged her to go...?). She didn't even want to come to the house, which turned me off, considering my husband and I had been first-time homebuyers a year before. She had originally told Avery to ask me if *I* could meet *her* in Delaware at her and Olivia's mobile home, even though BWI airport was only 20 minutes from me.

I held my ground. "Sorry, Avery, but I can't. Savannah is still in school and I have to wait for her to get off the school bus."

So poor Veronica was forced to see my new house, not being the least bit interested. But she did arrive with fresh caviar, kept cold inside a temperature-controlled lunch carrier. I'd never had caviar before but knew the *Osetra* had to be expensive, so I pulled the ceramic hors devours plates from the higher cabinets and lit some candles.

"Well, here's to your graduation," my mother calmly announced as she took a seat at the dining room table. "Congratulations on getting your master's." With a demure tip of her head towards me, she barely met my eyes. Instead, she began smoothing creme fraiche atop her *blini* before quietly tasting her appetizer.

"Thanks, Mom." My light tone matched hers, but my insides were quivering as I took the seat furthest from her at the dining table. I didn't know what else to say, and since the silence was more than I could bear I added, "Hopefully, I can go for my PhD soon."

"That's quite an endeavor," Veronica responded between bites of caviar. "I tip my mortarboard to you."

"Thank you."

"And the creme, Mom, it goes on like this...?" That was Avery, who watched my mother ever so closely from her spot right next to her. Apparently, she had never had caviar, either. Even though I always envied the relationship Avery had with our mother, I learned through my years to accept things for what they were, just grateful that she was there at the dining table with us as the buffer between me and Veronica.

"Well, yes, you just spread it on like this..." Veronica took her miniature appetizer knife and proceeded to show her youngest daughter how to properly prepare her *blini* for the Osetra.

"Avery, you can also use these little toasted mini breads." That was Olivia. I looked on as Olivia took one of the mini toasts out of a separate package and began adding her creme. "I usually prefer the toasts."

"Grandmother, do you have anything else for me to eat?"

That was Cody, my four-year-old, whose appetite was never satisfied.

"Oh, you want *more*?" My mother finished her bite, visibly delighted that Cody felt comfortable enough to approach her since meeting her for the very first time that day, feeling okay to ask for more goodies in addition to the chocolate she had given him 20 minutes before.

"Well let me see what I have." Veronica bent over and looked through her handbag that hung from her chair and began fishing for snacks. As Cody waited patiently by his grandmother, I looked towards three-year-old Matthew, who kept a comfortable distance from everyone as he remained on the sofa, still trying to figure everything out.

"Okay, well I found a pack of Oreos. Here you are, sweetie." I took a bite of my blini and watched as Cody took the cookies excitedly.

"Thank you, Grandmother!"

The Osetra was exquisite, but I ate very little as I sat in my corner of the dining area and just... observed.

• • •

I suddenly pulled my hand from Avery's chest as a thought occurred to me. I *was absolutely positive* she had been sick for a while; the confusion in her voice and her quick downhill battle told me as much. But had Veronica and Olivia known the whole time? I remembered the awkward pose I took as I stood next to Avery after we had all finally met in New Hampshire, dressed inside my black cap and gown, as she proudly stood next to Veronica while Olivia snapped a picture of us soon after I had walked across the stage and received my fourth degree. The air was light and breezy, and the sun shone brightly. New Hampshire was a little cold in May for my taste, but it had been an absolutely beautiful trip.

"This will probably be the last picture we take together," Veronica had declared before Olivia took the picture.

Weird. I couldn't even remember the last time the three of us stood together inside of any closed space, but she said nothing after that. I had figured that maybe my mother may have been sick in her older age, not *Avery*.

The last time I spoke to Avery was Christmas night. The little kids and I had celebrated Benjamin's thirteenth birthday a day early since Mateo wanted him for his *actual* birthday. We had Christmas gifts, cake, pizza, and lots of laughter. I had taken a video of him opening his gifts, which I subsequently texted to

Avery since she had not been able to make it. While I was driving Benjamin back to Mateo's, my sister had called me and it was the weirdest conversation:

Hi Megan! How are you?

Hi Avery! I'm okay. How are you?

Well, I'm okay!

Are you sure?

Well, yes!

Something was off, because she normally would have wished Benjamin a happy birthday right off the bat. But I went with it.

Great! But can I call you back in a few? I'm on the road taking Benjamin back to his dad's.

Oh yes. Sure!

Five minutes later, my phone rang again:

Hi Megan! How are you?

And that's when I knew something was definitely wrong.

Hey Avery! Let me call you back in about thirty minutes, is that okay?

Oh sure!

And that was it. To this day, the video of Benjamin's birthday party that I had texted to her during our celebration remains unread. Avery never got to view it, and I was never able to call her back.

• • •

The day before Avery passed, I received a text from Olivia, making sure that Veronica had no idea Dad had spent six hours with Avery the day before, while doctors ran the required tests to officially pronounce her brain dead. I was in complete awe that that would be one of the last things on her or Veronica's minds as Avery lied in wait of being permanently disconnected from life.

On New Year's day, Olivia let me know that Avery had passed the night before, on the last day of the previous year. I texted my Aunt Margaret, my dad's sister-in-law, to let her know about her niece, but the text accidentally went to my mother.

Hi Aunt Margaret. Just wanted to let you know Avery's last day was last night –

And then I stopped myself after realizing that I had texted Veronica by accident.

Megan, you texted me by mistake.

Yes, I'm sorry. But did Olivia let you know that Avery passed last night?

Nothing after that.

• • •

It has been thirteen months and six days since Avery passed. I'm not the same person I was two weeks ago as the barrage of epiphanies has been nothing short of jarring. But the most important and heart-stopping realization I received in the aftermath was that I will probably never receive the acceptance or love that I'd sought from Veronica for most of my life; whatever may have existed before more than likely died along with my sister. But as a mother of five, a wife, a person who was finally able to conquer her demons, and now an only child, what difference did it still make when I had a life to continue making for myself, and children still left to rear to the best of my ability? I'm not sure what I did to her, or what was done to *her* in her childhood. But what I'm finally sure of is that none of it had anything to do with me, and that I did deserve to have always known my value, my strength, and my abilities. And now, it was time to let go so I could make the room needed to create my own happiness.

I take shots of tequila as I think of Adam, Mateo, and all the other men I used to pursue in my desperate need to fill holes left in my heart from long ago. I was wrong, but the chase-rejection-*more chase* cycle was a game I had grown accustomed to as a child. For me, that *was* love. And that's why it was second nature for me to keep running behind men even after their repeated and blatant disrespect of me. It was nothing... but 'love.'

Since becoming an adult, I've had babies out of wedlock, lost infants when God was trying to warn me, started school, kept a longtime position, and finished school. I've gotten married and given birth to children *inside of wedlock*, purchased a home, and had my first essay published right before finishing my third degree. But through my sister's death, I finally understood that *none of those things* mattered to my mother, none of them. At close to middle age, I am still the same hated kid who Veronica despised. And it didn't hit me until my sister was on her deathbed, and the only thing my mother could think of doing was keeping my father and me out of the picture as she entrusted my sister's last wishes and arrangements to Olivia, someone who'd only been in Avery's life for ten or twelve years, nothing compared to the thirty-eight I had spent with her.

To this moment, I still have not heard from Veronica. I take another shot of tequila and unlock my phone's screen. I press *Delete Contact* under her name, and I keep moving forward.

Acknowledgments

First and foremost, thank you Father God, for sustaining me and my children through this extremely arduous but eye-opening journey. Thank you always for your sustenance, your faithfulness, your gifts, and your ongoing provision.

Secondly, I'd like to thank the family members, close friends, in-laws, and my *number one fan* who stood by me, made sure the children and I never starved, provided Christmas and birthday gifts throughout the years, cheered me on through school, my writing endeavors, my financial burdens, and made sure I had a nice bottle to keep me sane through the dark times. You know who you are. *Thank you.*

To Mr. Madramootoo, who traveled with me, dined with me, and made sure he was front and center for all of my writing and academic milestones, no matter how challenging situations became. *Thank you.*

To all of my children, for minding your mother whenever she needed peace and quiet to write and study... and for remaining steadfast and loyal whenever times got tough, *thank you.*

To *all* of my writing and English professors who guided me and watched me thrive as a student and writer, *thank you.*

To all of the cancer patients I cared for while keeping my head above water—you have given me *so much* to hold close to my heart until the end of my days. *Thank you.*

To the publishers, design team, editorial development, and promotional development teams at Apprentice House—thank you for your faith in my work and your professionalism in this process from acceptance to book design. And to my publicists at MindBuck Media—thank you for your creativity and expertise in providing my author's platform.

And lastly, a big thank you to the father of my oldest child. If you hadn't left me on the park bench that night, I wouldn't have this testimony to offer.

About the Author

Having begun *Not You* as part of her master's thesis while attending Southern New Hampshire University, Megan Harris M. is now working on her PhD in English, with a concentration in Creative Writing and a minor in Literary Theory at Morgan State University in Baltimore, MD. She also serves as an Instructor of Record for their Department of English. Her creative works usually include pieces of her past that she uses to help others who've experienced the same, as well as some academic projects that explore the lasting effects of colonialism and sexism. Megan resides in Maryland, just south of the city of Baltimore.

Apprentice
House Press
Loyola University Maryland

Apprentice House is the country's only campus-based, student-staffed book publishing company. Directed by professors and industry professionals, it is a nonprofit activity of the Communication Department at Loyola University Maryland.

Using state-of-the-art technology and an experiential learning model of education, Apprentice House publishes books in untraditional ways. This dual responsibility as publishers and educators creates an unprecedented collaborative environment among faculty and students, while teaching tomorrow's editors, designers, and marketers.

Eclectic and provocative, Apprentice House titles intend to entertain as well as spark dialogue on a variety of topics. Financial contributions to sustain the press's work are welcomed. Contributions are tax deductible to the fullest extent allowed by the IRS.

To learn more about Apprentice House books or to obtain submission guidelines, please visit www.apprenticehouse.com.

Apprentice House Press
Communication Department
Loyola University Maryland
4501 N. Charles Street
Baltimore, MD 21210
Ph: 410-617-5265
info@apprenticehouse.com • www.apprenticehouse.com

Printed in the USA
CPSIA information can be obtained
at www.ICGtesting.com
JSHW061952140224
57379JS00012B/63

9 781627 205320